A Window to the World

THE FIRST 100 YEARS
OF THE NATRONA COUNTY PUBLIC LIBRARY

BY

WALTER R. JONES

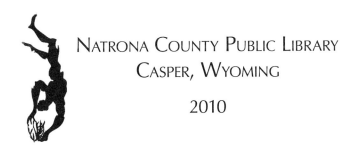

NATRONA COUNTY PUBLIC LIBRARY
CASPER, WYOMING

2010

Printed in the United States of America
by Mountain States Lithographing
Casper, Wyoming

International Standard Book Number 978-0-9769584-1-3

Published by the Natrona County Public Library

Table of Contents

Acknowledgments

This book is the product of the contributions of many people. First and greatest is the encouragement and assistance of the Natrona County Public Library Director, Bill Nelson, who conceived the history project and then continually inspired me to complete a manuscript for publication.

Next in line for praise are Nicholle Gerharter, Judith L. Highfill, Betsy O'Neil, April Szuch, and Brenda Thomson. These library employees formed an editorial team that spent many hours smoothing out the manuscript's narrative, suggesting illustrations to enhance the work, and finally acting as a liaison group with Mountain States Lithographing to offer advice and make decisions regarding format and layout of the ultimate publication. Their endeavors were essential to the success of the project.

A large number of others have contributed to this book. Among these were Trula Cooper, Beverly Diehl, Larry Diehl, Frank "Pinky" Ellis, Jackie Ellis, Jerry Hand, Agnes Hand, Jackie Read, Frank Schepis, Art Volk, and Jackie Volk, all of whom, through their willingness to share memories of the library, gave invaluable insights into the library's past. Either through email, telephone, or in person, they assisted in developing an understanding of people whose labors helped create a rich history of service and dedication to the library as an institution.

Still others assisted in administrative or research ways such as providing copying facilities, searching rolls of microfilm, and suggesting sources that would provide useful and fascinating information for the book. These include Kevin Anderson, Doug Cooper, Carol Crump, Greta Lehnerz, John Masterson, Bob Moore, Kate Mutch, Fred Parsons, Barbara Jay Penhallow, Becky Spahn, and Pamela Reamer Williams. In addition, Lesley Boughton, Sybil Dray, Vivian Holt, Helen Walker Jones, Beth Nelson, and Gregory C. Thompson took an active interest in the project to the extent that they provided much needed encouragement and support to me as the book took shape.

It is also appropriate and important to mention organizations and institutions whose influence helped make the project possible. These include the Natrona County Public Library's Board of Trustees, the Friends of the Library, the Natrona County Public Library Foundation, the Casper Area Community Foundation, the Natrona County Commission, the City of Casper, and the Natrona County Historical Society. All of these groups deserve my gratitude for their active involvement in projects and functions that have made the Natrona County Public Library a success story worthy of a centennial history book.

Although I have already mentioned her once, I would like to repeat my praise for my wife, Helen Walker Jones. She has always supported me in whatever historic subject I have studied from the early days of our marriage when I was obsessed with the history of Casper's Sand Bar district, to the more recent studies of Evanston, Wyoming's oil fields and now this library history. It is always impressive to read other acknowledgments and to learn how much a person's spouse can contribute to a researcher's endeavors.

Finally, I wish to apologize in advance if I have forgotten to mention anyone whose work has assisted in completing the history of the Natrona County Public Library. Experience has taught me that in my imperfect state of being, I sometimes suffer memory lapses that I sincerely wish I would not have to endure. This said, however, I am grateful to all who have made the book possible.

Preface

It is a privilege to serve as the Natrona County Public Library Director and in so doing foster literacy and education as community values. It is even more of a privilege to be Director as this institution celebrates its hundredth anniversary. My predecessors have done an admirable job in bringing library service to our community. Some have been agents of change, while others simply did their best to keep a sinking vessel afloat. Regardless, the people of Natrona County have faithfully used this library to introduce their children to reading, for homework, to start businesses, to learn about the world, or simply to enjoy the latest western or mystery novel.

The library began as a modest Carnegie library serving through Wyoming's booms and busts, two world wars, the Great Depression, and the rise and fall of Casper as the oil capital of the Rockies. Throughout these periods, citizens have used the Natrona County Public Library for research, recreation, entertainment, and business purposes. As the population grew, the Library Board and County Commissioners expanded the facility three times in order to accommodate demand. The materials librarians offered to our citizens likewise changed. In 1910, the materials were solely books, manuscripts, and newsprint. This later changed to include microfilm, vinyl LP records, artwork, toys, cassettes, VHS tapes, and now CD-ROM, DVDs, MP3s, and computer software. One can only imagine what formats will be circulating from the Natrona County Public Library when the community celebrates its 200th anniversary in 2110!

In 1910, Casper was in many ways an island of people, isolated by geography. It is not hard to understand why our early county and city leaders recognized the service that a library would provide in connecting local citizens with "outside" information, new ideas, and the latest books and regional newspapers. Over the years Natrona County's connectedness with the world has improved to the point that it is now seamless. News, information, and books are available from nearly any part of the world in Casper in real time. Nevertheless, the fundamental function of providing economical connectedness for every citizen continues to be something the Natrona County Public Library accomplishes every day. And we continue to be the place where Natrona County citizens connect with the information they seek.

Librarians have a saying, "The easiest place to lose a book is in a library." This refers to the fact that mis-shelved books are often difficult to locate. While librarians work to organize and access our holdings as easily as possible, like many professionals, we often focus on our customers while leaving a less than tidy trail of our own organization's history. Such was the case at the Natrona County Public Library. Remnants of our history were "lost" within our own walls. Walter Jones has done our community a great service by helping to organize and preserve the history of this grand institution.

About ten years ago, the Natrona County Public Library's organizational records, memory books, plaques, and memorabilia were strewn throughout the building and community. Over the past decade it has been thrilling to move piles of things in the basement only to realize they had been hiding plaques from the early 1920s or scrapbooks from the 1960s. Annual reports were likewise tucked away in various corners of the facility…and were nearly thrown out with other detritus. When discovered, all of these items were placed in a central location with the hope that one day they might be organized and preserved. Walter Jones has helped us to preserve and weave the story that these documents have hidden for many years.

I got to know Walter Jones quite by accident several years ago. Not having grown up in Casper and wanting to learn its history, I read Walter's first book, *The Sand Bar*. Our librarians and I surmised Walter must be a sage citizen who might have already passed on to the next world. Much to my pleasant surprise, I received an unannounced visitor on June 14, 2001. It was none other than a young Walter Jones. We had a wonderful discussion about his time as a Natrona County Public Library reference librarian between August 1973 and March 1976 and his current position as Assistant Head of Special Collections at the University of Utah in Salt Lake City. Our mutual military service sealed a personal friendship that continues to this day.

In 2005, as we began to anticipate our upcoming hundredth anniversary, the concept of writing a history book about this library began to get legs. As Walter was concluding his second book, *Derricks and Determination,* he responded to our request to write the Natrona County Public Library's history. Declining a fee, he looked at this effort as a labor of love and gift to his hometown library. We are most grateful to Walter for his commitment to Natrona County and for developing this book.

It is my hope that you will discover new connections in which your Natrona County Public Library has helped our community grow while serving thousands of citizens over the past century. Public libraries, by their nature, must serve the enduring needs of their communities. This requires that library boards and staffs consciously engage their communities. I think you will find that the Natrona County Public Library has a long and proven history of doing just that. By adjusting the collection to the needs of booms and busts, and continually fostering literacy and education, the Natrona County Public Library has a distinguished history of service.

As we look back at the past one hundred years, we are also looking forward to a much different world, but one in which people will still need access to early literacy books, authoritative information, and the pleasure that comes from a variety of good books. I imagine it will be interesting for librarians to read this document one hundred years from now to compare how they have adjusted to the needs of our citizens as well as new methods to deliver materials to their patrons. While the librarian's fundamental roles will likely be unchanged, this book will provide a benchmark to chronicle how things were done in the old times of 2010.

Bill Nelson
Casper, Wyoming
2010

Chapter One: Planting the Seeds for a Carnegie Library

*Casper ... is the county seat, has many good business blocks
and nice residences and is a permanent town. We not only have
an assured future but are distinctly of the present.*

Wilson S. Kimball, Mayor of Casper, 1903-1913

When the early waves of pioneers moved west across the continent, they generally passed by the high plains and Rocky Mountains seeking greener pastures and the promised wealth of the gold fields. However, over the years settlements sprang up along the trails at forts and river crossings. With the coming of the railroads, large-scale ranching on the

*Roads in town were little better than in the oil fields when freight outfits made the haul in to early Casper refineries.
Undated photo by W. G. Passmore, courtesy Casper College Western History Center, Sheffner-McFadden Collection.*

plains became profitable. Valuable ores and oil were discovered, and hardy homesteaders staked out farms. In April 1889, the collection of homes and businesses that had grown up near the Platte Bridge Station officially became the Town of Casper. The next year, Casper became the county seat of the newly created Natrona County in the recently ratified state of Wyoming. According to federal Census records, in 1890 there were 1,100 people living in Natrona County with only 540 in Casper.

At the beginning of the twentieth century, Natrona County, Wyoming, was still a rugged frontier province. By 1900, the population of the county had grown to 1,800 and Casper's population was 880. The region's single railroad provided only freight service, rural life was harsh, and the roads were miserable. Often early settlers in isolated places like Wolton, west of Casper, lived in sheepherder's wagons, tents, or one-room log cabins with dirt roofs. Unimproved roads such as the one crossing Tank Farm Hill, on the trail north of Casper leading to the Salt Creek Oil Field camps, were so muddy that strings of freight wagons had to be uncoupled and dragged one by one to the top of the hill.

During the first decade of the twentieth century, however, living conditions began to improve. Natrona County and its county seat, Casper, began to appear permanent and prosperous, reflecting the energies, talents, and civic-minded nature of the region's persistent citizens. A flourishing ranching industry contributed to the growth of a center for support services and transportation. From the beginning of the region's settlement, the county had been an attractive place to raise both cattle and sheep. Irving Garbutt, in *Casper Centennial,* writes, "In 1888, the sheepman also awoke to the fact that Natrona County grass was pretty good for sheep as well as cattle." He notes further that within the first twenty years of the

twentieth century, raising livestock became a major industry for the county.

A second element in assuring Natrona County's economic and cultural growth was the expansion of the rail system. In 1903, the Fremont, Elkhorn, & Missouri Valley Railroad resumed passenger service to Casper, a service that it had offered in the late 1880s and abandoned in 1892. Then, in the spring of 1905, the Chicago & North Western Railroad, the parent company of the Fremont, Elkhorn, & Missouri Valley Railroad and the Wyoming Central, began extending its line through the county toward Lander, Wyoming. This was a major impetus to one of Natrona County's important enterprises, wool growing, and factored into the economic well-being of the entire region. A news item in the December 14, 1905, issue of the *Natrona County Tribune* detailed the first livestock shipment, which was loaded just west of Casper and bound for South Omaha, Nebraska. The article also stated that Casper had recently become a maintenance center for the railroad company, which meant that the heads of twenty-four families had moved to Casper with others to follow.

Another sign of Natrona County's improved economic condition was the success that oilmen were achieving in the county's Salt Creek Oil Field. In 1890, Philip Martin Shannon had become successful enough to form the Pennsylvania Oil and Gas Company and to build a small refinery in Casper near South Center Street. In 1901, a group of European entrepreneurs, having formed a partnership called the Wyoming Syndicate, began to negotiate with Shannon to purchase his refinery and oil lands. One of these men, Joseph Lobell of London, England, then began to work the properties to the extent that on March 16, 1905, the *Natrona County Tribune* announced hopefully, "Six New Oil Wells: J. S. Lobell Will Commence at Once to Improve His Natrona County Property."

The article stated that Lobell planned to drill many other wells before the end of the year.

Despite the optimistic reporting of the *Tribune* in 1905, the real launch of Natrona County's oil industry took place in 1908 when a Dutch petroleum company led by Coenraad Kerbert hired H. E. "Daddy" Stock and his son Jim Stock to drill a well at Salt Creek. In October of that year, the Stocks struck a gusher known as Wall Creek No. 1. This ignited the imaginations of many oil speculators who began to form drilling companies, buying and selling stock at Casper's Grand Central Hotel on Center Street.

Given Casper's improved rail service and the county's sheep and cattle industries, as well as the discoveries at the Salt Creek Oil Field, it is not surprising that Natrona County began to experience solid growth in the first years of the twentieth century. Again, the *Natrona County Tribune* heralded the quickening pace of the area's growth. A February 17, 1907, news article declared, "The year 1907 will be the banner building year for Casper. Already arrangements

Rail transportation was essential to the growth of western communities. This Chicago & North Western passenger train arrived in Casper circa 1912.
Photo by Wiswall (Denver), courtesy Casper College Western History Center, Frances Seely Webb Collection.

have been made for the construction of public buildings and new business blocks which will cost more than $150,000."

One of the two most iconic buildings to be constructed during Natrona County's transition from frontier status to a place of modern, urban character was a courthouse. The other important building was the public library. County residents first began to lobby for a courthouse building in early 1906. On a late winter day that year, Patrick Sullivan, W. A. Blackmore, C. M. Elgin, Oscar Heistand, and E. F. Seaver, members of the Casper Boosters,

met with the County Commissioners, L. L. Gantz, Charles C. P. Webel, and C. A. Hall, to request the building of a courthouse that would reflect the increasing affluence of their county. Agreeing with the Boosters, the Commissioners decided to hold a bond election to raise $40,000 to erect the new county facility. This bond issue passed in November 1906, by a vote of 680 to 140.

The County Commissioners began by employing Casper's only architect, C. A. Randall, to design the courthouse and by hiring the firm of Schmidt & Esmay of Douglas,

Early in the twentieth century the intersection of Second and Center streets was already the business hub of Casper. This undated photo looks east on Second Street with the Townsend Building (still standing today) on the left. Photo by Wiswall (Denver), courtesy Casper College Western History Center, Frances Seely Web Collection.

Natrona County's courthouse stood at the end of North Center Street, approximately where the street passes under the railroad tracks today, and faced south.
Undated photo, courtesy Wyoming State Archives and Historical Department.

Wyoming, to build it. As work began, however, heated debate evolved over the courthouse's site at the north end of Center Street. Before selecting this location, the Commissioners held a special meeting to seek public input into three proposed sites. Local historian Alfred James Mokler elaborates in his *History of Natrona County, Wyoming, 1888-1922:*

> A great many people were present at this meeting and some heated argument was indulged in. Petitions were presented favoring the three sites, and after patiently listening to the argument, carefully perusing the petitions and diligently studying the situation from every angle,

it was decided the north Center street site was the one favored by the greatest number of taxpayers, and the commissioners unanimously decided that this was where the building should be.

This location, straddling Center Street, angered a very vocal Casperite named Silas Adsit. He protested that the site was too sandy, windblown, and subject to flooding from the North Platte River. Despite Adsit's legal maneuvers and the concerns of others who were initially unhappy with the site, construction proceeded. On June 22, 1908, officials from the city's Masonic Lodge laid the building's cornerstone.

Wilson S. Kimball was Casper's Mayor from 1903 to 1913 and a driving force in the campaign to build a community library.
Undated photo, courtesy Casper College Western History Center.

On February 10, 1909, the county's new courthouse was completed. For $44,300, the residents of Natrona County now had a Classical Revival style structure that featured an exterior fashioned from Omaha brick and white sandstone, an elegantly domed roof, and a seven-foot-tall statue of Lady Justice. (Today this statue adorns the lobby of the current courthouse on North Center Street.) By 1910 the population of Natrona County had reached 4,800 and Casper's population had grown to 2,700, nearly tripled from ten years earlier.

The second major building to reflect Natrona County's progress in the first decade of the twentieth century was the public library. The history of the library actually began eight years before the building was erected. In November 1903, the County Commissioners created the Natrona County Public Library

Association with F. E. Matheny, N. S. Bristol, and Wilson S. Kimball as the first three Trustees. Their mission was to manage the affairs of a very simple library, which consisted of a collection of books formerly managed by a local segment of the Women's Christian Temperance Union (WCTU). According to Mokler's *History of Natrona County,* in the autumn of 1902 the WCTU had created a library that "occupied some shelves in a small building located on the east side of Center street, between Second and First." After taking charge of this institution, the Natrona County Public Library Association obtained from the County Commissioners a commitment to provide an annual appropriation for their library. Mokler described the Association's book collection as nonsectarian, nonpolitical, and of the type that would "inform the mind and improve the character of the reader." No more than 25 percent of the collection could be fiction, and all items were to be lent to the county's citizens without charge.

Most prominent of the Association's three Trustees was Wilson S. Kimball, Mayor of the Town of Casper during that first decade of the twentieth century. Kimball was extremely active in the region's business, civic, and political affairs. Born in New Hampshire in 1866, he moved with his parents to Wyoming, then traveled to Illinois to marry Edness Merrick in 1887. Returning to Wyoming, he worked for a newspaper in Glenrock until, according to the book *Progressive Men of the State of Wyoming,* "Leading citizens of the brisk city of Casper, persuaded him to establish a newspaper plant in their midst."

Once in Casper, he became a guiding force. First, he assisted in establishing the newspaper *Wyoming Derrick.* Then he became a woolgrower, acquiring 480 acres of land on the North Platte River, six miles east of Casper, near the site of the current Edness Kimball Wilkins

State Park, named for his daughter. In addition, he bought into a drugstore partnership, ultimately owning his own business selling drugs, paints, oils, glass and jewelry. His enterprise employed a jeweler and watch-repairer and several clerks.

Kimball was an Episcopalian who obtained the position of vestryman. He was the town's treasurer and then served as Mayor from 1903 to 1913. He also volunteered on the town's fire department, played in the municipal brass band, joined the city's Masonic Order where he was a Knight Templar, and became a member of the Commercial Club. It was during his tenure as Mayor that he became a member of the Natrona County Public Library Association's Trustees. Of his various achievements, *Progressive Men of the State of Wyoming* comments, "He has been conspicuous among his associates, not only for his success, but for his probity, fairness, honorable methods and unbounded energy."

WILSON S. KIMBALL
DRUGS AND JEWELRY
TOILET ARTICLES, FANCY GOODS, ETC.
CASPER, WYOMING

6/12/05

PAINTS, OILS, GLASS, WALL PAPER
KODAKS PHONOGRAPHS
CIGARS, CANDIES, NEWS STAND

Andrew Carnegie,
New York City.

Dear Sir:--I am directed by the Town Council and upon the request of a number of our citizens (including the Ministers and Principal of Schools), to address to you this formal application for the erection of a Carnegie Library in Casper.

We have a town here of at the present time about 1500 population and there is probably not a more cosmopolitan town, of its size, in the United States. This is essientially a range live-stock country, in which many men are constantly going to and coming from town. A Carnegie Library here would benefit a class thet are seldom benefitted by such institutions, and would afford a quiet, wholesome and instructive resort of a character that are too scarce in these western range towns.

Casper has a $50,000 gravity system of water-works, supplying pure mountain water; a modern electric lighting plant, a sanitary sewer aystem costing $16,000, complete telephone connections with all portions of the country, the town is the county seat, has many good business blocks and nice residences and is a permanent town . We not only have an Assured future but are distinctly of the present.
Very Truly Yours,
Mayor.

A copy of the original letter Mayor Kimball sent to Andrew Carnegie, requesting funds to build the first public library for Natrona County.
Letter from NCPL files.

Given Kimball's energy and devotion to the city, it is appropriate that he would be the guiding light in pursuing the construction of a public library building for Casper and Natrona County. As Mayor, he wrote to Andrew Carnegie on June 12, 1905, to request money to build a Carnegie library. In his letter he detailed how the town and its surrounding region had progressed from a frontier wilderness to a place possessing an "assured future." He emphasized that a library "would afford a quiet, wholesome and instructive resort of a character that are too scarce in these western range towns."

Chapter Two: Firm Foundations

1906-1929

A public library is a never-failing spring in the desert.

Andrew Carnegie

Andrew Carnegie had been engaged in donating money for the construction of public libraries for nearly twenty years when Casper Mayor Wilson S. Kimball first wrote to him in 1905. Theodore Jones, author of *Carnegie Libraries Across America: A Public Legacy*, called the industrialist's library program "the most influential philanthropic program in American history." Before this program ended in 1919, Carnegie had given $41.5 million (approximately $1.1 billion in terms of 2010 dollars) to assist in the building of 1,700 public libraries throughout the United States. Of that sum, Wyoming communities would receive $257,500 to build a total of sixteen public libraries between 1899 and 1917.

Cheyenne held the honor of being Wyoming's first city to benefit from the Carnegie library program when the benefactor awarded it $50,000 in December 1899. At the time, the population of Cheyenne was approximately 14,000. Laramie, Evanston, Sheridan, and Green River followed before Casper's Mayor sent his letter in 1905 requesting funds for a library. Lander, Rock Springs, Basin, Buffalo, Newcastle, Cody, Lusk, Wheatland, and Thermopolis all received grants by the end of April 1917.

Carnegie hired James Bertram at the end of 1897 to supervise the daily operations of his international library-gift program. One of Bertram's duties was to handle a deluge of mail regarding requests for donations to communities that wished to construct public libraries. It was

Bertram who answered, sometimes bluntly, all correspondence from Casper, Natrona County, and Wyoming representatives during the years that city, county, state, and even federal officials carried on a lively written dialogue over the amount of money Casper was ultimately to receive. Bertram also held Casper accountable for

Andrew Carnegie (1835-1919) circa 1913. Libraries were not the only educational endeavors funded by Carnegie, who believed it was his duty to share his wealth.
Photoprint copyright Marceau (New York City), courtesy Library of Congress Prints and Photographs Division, Washington, D.C.

meeting all of the Carnegie library program's requirements, such as providing a building site and guaranteeing an ongoing annual appropriation equal to 10 percent of Carnegie's gift for the operation and maintenance of the library. Casper's Town Council agreed to these stipulations.

Letters for the Library

All communities with a population of 1,000 or more residents qualified for Carnegie's consideration for grant money. In his first letter, Mayor Kimball stated that Casper had a population of 1,500 residents. Six months later, Wyoming Governor Bryant B. Brooks wrote to

Senator Joseph M. Carey, 1892. Four years after providing a building site for the future Natrona County Public Library, Carey became Wyoming's Governor and later a U.S. Senator.
Photo by C. M. Bell, courtesy Casper College Western History Center, David Memorial Collection.

Carnegie to confirm Casper's population and its progressive nature. On February 13, 1906, Bertram sent Kimball the news that "Mr. Carnegie will be glad to give you Ten Thousand Dollars." To show compliance with the gift's stipulations of providing a building site and ongoing funding for the library, Casper's town clerk, M. P. Wheeler, replied on April 5, 1906, that the town had passed a resolution to provide $1,000 yearly for "the maintenance of a free public library." He added, however, a request that Carnegie's gift be increased to $20,000. Wheeler then followed up with a letter on April 14 to inform Bertram that Joseph M. Carey of Cheyenne had donated land for the library. In this second correspondence, he asked, "What do you think about increasing your gift to $15,000?" Bertram replied that Casper officials could call upon R. A. Franks, Carnegie's financial manager, for sums as needed up to $10,000.

Having secured a grant, Casper's representatives hired architect C. A. Randall to design the library building. Randall designed a one-story brick and stone structure with one large and two small white domes and a wide set of stairs leading to an elaborate entryway set off by two large Ionic pillars. Set high off the ground, the building would have a full basement to augment the rooms on the first level. Randall's design reflected an architectural pattern that has become known as Carnegie Classic and represents nearly one-quarter of the 1,689 Carnegie libraries in the United States. With some exceptions, such as the lack of a pediment over the entryway, Casper's design was similar to the $10,000 Ladysmith, Wisconsin, library built in 1907 that Theodore Jones's book describes as Carnegie Classic "with its half-exposed foundation of rusticated stone, brick walls with corners accented by quoins, a pediment supported by only two engaged Ionic columns, large windows on either side of the entrance, and high windows ringing the other three elevations."

In late September 1906, Charles Galusha received the contract to build the city's new facility. His bid price was $10,400, an amount that soon proved to be insufficient to comply with Randall's blueprints. By late July 1907, Mayor Kimball and his Town Councilmen were forced to inform Carnegie that they would need additional funds to finish their building. Randall suggested that due to "extra work and prices," the amount needed was now $4,200. He also claimed that the original contract cost of $10,400 did not include finishing the basement or installing heating, plumbing, electrical wiring, and fixtures, or putting in sidewalks and curbs. Further, Randall added that a local cement block company had failed to provide blocks of the same quality as the samples the firm had shown the architect. Therefore, Randall declared, he and the Mayor had decided on sandstone blocks from Hot Springs, South Dakota; this decision added $690 to the cost of construction.

Governor Brooks supported Casper's Mayor and Council in a letter to Carnegie in which he complimented the appearance of the yet-to-be-finished library. He declared it was a "splendid library building, one of the most attractive I have ever seen."

Bertram, however, was not impressed. Writing to M. P. Wheeler on August 27, 1907, he announced, "Mr. Carnegie does not see his way to add to the amount promised because he considers it ample for the erection of an adequate library building for Casper."

In trouble, Kimball wrote to Wyoming's United States Congressman Frank W. Mondell to enlist his support to obtain the extra funds. He admitted in a letter to Mondell on January 8,

SKIBO CASTLE,
DORNOCH,
SUTHERLAND.

August 27th, 1907.

M. P. Wheeler, Esq.,
    Town Clerk, Casper, Wyo.

Dear Sir,

    Yours of July 23rd received.   Mr. Carnegie does not see his way to add to the amount promised because he considers it ample for the erection of an adequate Library Building for Casper.   With regard to the rise in price of materials etc., there has been no rise in these of any moment since the Library Building was promised.

                    Respectfully yours,

                    Jas Bertram

                            P. Secretary.

Correspondence and negotiations with the Carnegie Foundation were handled by James Bertram.
Letter from Bertram dated 1907 from NCPL files.

1908, "We have a most creditable structure, albeit somewhat more imposing than should have been undertaken with the amount of money at our disposal." In response to Mondell's appeal on behalf of Casper's library, Bertram declared that a blunder had been made. Persisting, Mondell wrote that the new building was handsome, thoroughly well-built, and "splendidly located." Even though he confessed that there was no justification for going beyond the monies authorized, he said that Casper's officials would be hard-put to provide the amount needed to finish the building.

At this point, Governor Brooks became involved again. Bertram stated curtly in a letter to Brooks that the people of Casper knew "perfectly well" that they would only receive $10,000. He concluded, stating that Mr. Carnegie "is indisposed to provide further funds." Bertram then wrote to a prominent Casper attorney,

Alex Butler, on January 11, 1909, "In the case of the Casper building, it is a case of deliberately ignoring the resources provided." Yet a few days later he informed Kimball that Mr. Carnegie would be glad to provide $3,000 if the Council would guarantee an extra $300 per year for the maintenance of the library. Bertram explained to Brooks that the Governor's urgent appeal had caused Mr. Carnegie to make available the extra funds.

Between the time when Bertram told Casper's representatives about the additional $3,000 and the time he wrote to Governor Brooks regarding Carnegie's change of mind, the city admitted that it could not provide an annual appropriation of $1,300 to support the library. This being the case, the County Commission accepted responsibility for maintaining the library. In April 1909, months before the city surrendered its claim to library ownership, the county reactivated the Natrona County Public Library Association and appointed Charles H. Townsend, Charles C. P. Webel, and John E. Schulte to that Board. In August 1909, Webel resigned his Board seat, and Harold Banner took his place as Secretary. On March 5, 1910, Banner wrote to Bertram to announce, "The board has been, and is doing all that is possible to open the Carnegie library at the very earliest opportunity which will probably be about the middle of May."

> ## Spotlight: 1910
> Natrona County Population: 4,800
> Casper Population: 2,700
>
> **Natrona County Public Library Facts**
> Head Librarian: Sarah E. Place
> Library Collection: 850
> Circulation: Between 1,000 and 2,800
> Budget: $2,000
> Board Members: Harold Banner,
>   John E. Schulte,
>   Charles H. Townsend

Funding and the Grand Opening

To make good on the library's construction debts, the Commissioners provided $2,500 that had been built up over the years from a mill levy earmarked for a library in order to stimulate the construction of such a facility. Although the money remained in the bank for the library, it had not been used because of the several-year delay in beginning the project. By Wyoming statutes, the county could not expend tax revenues to finish the building, but the state's Attorney General suggested that the Library Board could legally use its funds to repair the building. As quoted in Alfred J. Mokler's *History of Natrona County,*

The original Carnegie library in Casper faced Second Street and exemplified the Carnegie Classic style. Photo from NCPL files.

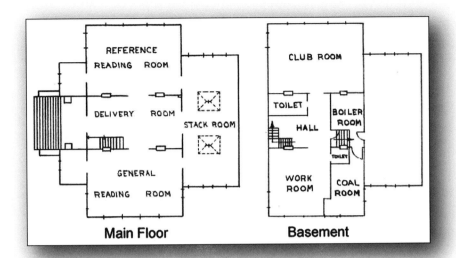

REFERENCE READING ROOM

DELIVERY ROOM

STACK ROOM

GENERAL READING ROOM

Main Floor

CLUB ROOM

TOILET

BOILER ROOM

HALL

TOILET

WORK ROOM

COAL ROOM

Basement

The floor plan of the original library building was simple and provided a meeting place for residents.
Plans dated 1910 from NCPL files.

the Attorney General declared, "If sentiment of the community is in favor of using the tax fund for completing the building, I would not suppose there would be any serious objections." Thus advised, the county pursued finishing the building.

When the Carnegie library was nearly complete, city and county officials held an open house to celebrate the five years of work involved in creating a free public library. The ceremony took place on Friday, May 20, 1910, and began with a reception from 8:30 to 9:30 p.m. at the library. Three hundred people were present, including Mayor Wilson S. Kimball and Library Board Chairman John

E. Schulte, both of whom spoke briefly. The Casper Concert Band performed and the community's Civic Club served ice cream, lemonade, and cake. Then a dance took place until 1:00 a.m. Cut flowers, a rarity in Casper at that time, adorned the library. Library officials raised one hundred dollars for the library's fund by charging a fee of one dollar per person for the evening's refreshments and dance.

Although the library opened its doors for business on Saturday, May 21, 1910, much work still needed to be accomplished to complete the structure and its surroundings. The Board had a little more than $3,000 for tying up loose ends from the construction project

LIBRARY OPENING

The formal opening of the Carnegie Library in Casper will occur on Friday evening of this week. The ladies of the Civic Club will have the affair in charge. There will be a reception and general program from 8:30 to 9:30, to be followed by a dance in all of the three commodious rooms. Refreshments will also be served. The reception is free and all are cordially invited. Tickets for the dance will be sold at $1.00, by the ladies who are endeavoring to raise some much needed funds for the library committee.

At the time of the library's opening ceremony, both interior and exterior details were still being completed.
Announcement for the 1910 opening ceremony originally published in the Natrona County Tribune, *May 18, 1910.*
Reprinted with permission from the Casper Star-Tribune.

and for operating the library for the rest of the calendar year. Of this money, nearly $2,000 went to obtaining furniture, installing lights, heat, and water, and doing concrete work. The rest of the funds helped pay ongoing expenses such as the librarian's salary, electricity, coal, books and magazines, and custodial work. Civic-minded citizens assisted in cleaning up the rubbish after the construction work, installing light fixtures and the furnace, and placing the concrete sidewalks. Civic Club members, Town Councilmen, Library Trustees, and other public-spirited citizens labored to see that all of the library's projects were done before the approach of autumn. This community involvement highlighted the public nature of the new Natrona County Public Library.

In common with frontier teachers, Sarah Place, Natrona County's first Head Librarian, had to wear many hats in her position.
Photo from NCPL files.

Key Figures at the Library

The Library Board selected Sarah E. Place from five candidates to manage the new facility. Place was born in New York in 1867 and moved to Ferris, Wyoming, in 1885. She married Casper pioneer Fred Place and moved to Casper in 1902, where they raised seven children. According to the library's 1960 annual report, she was an "industrious woman" who not only functioned as the county's librarian but also served as janitor. Her salary was set at fifty dollars per month when she first began her duties in 1910.

During Place's initial year at the new Natrona County Public Library, she kept the library open seven hours a day. However, records do not indicate whether the library offered simply Monday through Friday hours or was also open on weekends. She registered 200 borrowers, spent $300 for books, and lent somewhere between 1,000 and 2,800 items to her patrons. There is some disagreement about the number of books lent. Mokler in *History of Natrona County* states that the library's patrons borrowed 1,000 while the library's first annual report, dated January 17, 1911, gave a figure of 2,800. Regardless of which figure is more accurate, the numbers represent a modest beginning for the library. Casper merchant J. W. "Billy" Johnson, reflecting on Place's first year on the job, praised her for doing "a wonderful job of getting the library started."

Billy Johnson was in a good position to evaluate Place's contributions because he had become a member of the Library Board of Trustees in April 1918, after Harold Banner resigned his Board position to move to California. Johnson, like Place, was a transplant to Casper, having moved to the town in 1908 from Lincoln, Nebraska. First he managed the Webel Commercial Company, and then he went into business with George Campbell. The Campbell-Johnson Company sold

Looking northward at the back of businesses along Second Street. This early photo shows the rural nature of the town and its library when Place was librarian. The rear of the original library building and a hint of its distinctive white dome are visible in the upper right corner.
Photo from NCPL files.

clothing and related items. In 1935, Johnson opened his own business, a clothing store at 221 South Center Street. Years later, he commented about his coming to Casper, "I arrived in Casper in 1908 and the [library] building was not quite complete." Johnson remained on the Library Board until March 1965, when, after forty-seven years of service, he earned the distinction of being the longest-serving member in the library's history.

By 1918, the library had added Wilma Shaffner as assistant librarian and George Townsend as a custodian. Place's salary at that time was $80 per month. In April 1919, Place became ill and Shaffner became the acting librarian. Place died on May 3, 1919. Her obituary in the *Casper Daily Tribune* on May 5, 1919, read, "Mrs. Place has endeared herself to scores of local residents through her unfailing good humor and courtesy while serving in the capacity of librarian." Echoing Billy Johnson's appraisal, the *Tribune*'s comment suggests that Place succeeded in making the library a valuable and appreciated asset to the residents of Natrona County.

The county's second Head Librarian, Effie Rodgers, took advantage of boom times to increase her staff and concentrated on children's services.
Photo from NCPL files.

Effie Rodgers became the second Head Librarian. A native of Sydney, Nebraska, she came to Casper in 1901, where she taught school and married Ira H. Rodgers, a Casper pharmacist. At the time of her employment as librarian, Natrona County was undergoing an oil boom that was affecting the whole region. Circulation statistics demonstrate a tremendous increase in library use during this boom period. In 1914, for instance, the library circulated 12,300 items. By the end of 1922, that number had jumped to 74,200. The number continued to increase to more than 175,000 in 1929. In the 1920s, the library began to differentiate and record the types of materials that patrons were borrowing. For instance, the 1929 figure of approximately 175,000 items included nearly 110,000 adult books, 45,000 juvenile volumes, and 20,000 books "lent through school district collections."

Growth was the situation that challenged Rodgers during her tenure at the Natrona County Public Library. Budgets increased from approximately $2,000 spent in 1910 to approximately $3,000 until the early 1920s, then to more than $20,000 by the mid-1920s and to $33,200 in 1929. In 1919, Rodgers received a salary of $80 per month. This increased to $170 by 1926, when the library was paying a total of $430 per month to four full-time employees.

Spotlight: 1920
Natrona County Population: 14,600
Casper Population: 11,400

Natrona County Public Library Facts
Head Librarian: Effie Cummings
   Rodgers
Library Collection: 14,000
Circulation: 74,000
Budget: $20,000
Board Members: J. W. "Billy" Johnson,
   Charles H. Townsend

Growth in the Library Collection

The library's book and magazine collections continued to grow. From 850 books in 1910, the collection increased slowly to 3,600 items in 1915. In the 1920s, under Rodgers's administration, the collection grew more rapidly, to 14,400 in 1923 and to 21,000 in 1924. By 1929 the total stood at nearly 30,000. At the same time, Natrona County was experiencing a population explosion. Census records for 1910 indicate that the county was home to 4,800 residents, increasing to 14,600 in 1920 and then to 24,300 in 1930. Casper's population increased accordingly, from 2,700 in 1910 to 11,400 in 1920 and 16,600 in 1930.

On January 4, 1925, a *Casper Daily Tribune* article on the status of the library and its collections reflected the institution's growth. Noting the increased demand for books on subjects such as travel, essays, poetry, history, drama, and general reference, the paper quoted Rodgers as saying, "We feel we are more nearly reaching the goal of making our reading inspirational and educational as well as recreational." The news article also listed popular magazines, including *National Geographic, Literary Digest, Scribners,* and *Atlantic Monthly.* The library had 150 magazine and newspaper subscriptions. The collection grew in conjunction with extended library hours. The newspaper commented, "These [collections] give enjoyment to the reading public every day in the year; the reading rooms being kept open on Sundays and holidays as well as all week days."

An interesting illustration of the growth and use of the library's collections was reflected in the community's interest in Alfred J. Mokler's *History of Natrona County.* This volume was first published in 1923, and the library quickly acquired a copy. On February 6, 1927, the *Casper Tribune Herald* reported that the Natrona County Public Library owned six copies. "Even now," the paper stated, "these half dozen copies always have a waiting list."

Another demonstration of how important the public library was becoming to the county's residents was the frequent use of the library's meeting room. On January 4, 1925, the *Casper Daily Tribune*, explained the increased use of this room: "The assembly room in the basement is open to the public for meetings at any time conforming to library hours and fills a real need in the community. It is used almost every day for club meetings, committee meetings, debate work, and children's story hour programs."

Expanded Services to Children

Effie Rodgers expanded two programs to meet the growing needs of library patrons. The first was services to the children who visited the library. In 1922, the library hired its first children's librarian, Francis Giblin. Estella B. Houghton replaced Giblin in 1925. In the late 1920s, Cathryn Coale, who had worked for several years as a part-time employee, replaced Houghton. In the early 1920s, the library established a children's

room where, in Mokler's words, "There are many carefully selected books and pictures, with stereopticon views."

The children's librarian then began to attract young audiences to various story hour programs, which included a Christmas tree program for the Yule holiday and a "Twilight Story Hour" session held in conjunction with National Book Week. Again, Mokler surveyed the situation in 1921: "The children's story hour is made most interesting and instructive by well-trained story tellers." The library's 1928 annual report gave a clear idea of the popularity of the story-telling program: "Story hour was begun in June, with an average attendance of about twenty-four during the summer. This number increased rapidly after school began until by October, an attendance of around 200 made a division of the group necessary." The report continued, "Cathryn Coale, children's librarian, tells stories to the younger children at ten each Saturday morning, and to the older group at eleven."

Within two decades of the library's construction, it was surrounded by a rapidly growing city. Looking southeast from Second and Wolcott, the Carnegie dome can be seen beyond the post office and the telephone building.
Undated photo courtesy Casper College Western History Center, Holt-Gray Collection.

Also in 1928, the Trustees hired Eleanor Davis to replace Elva Randa, who had become the Acting Head Librarian after Rodgers died in June 1927. The same year, Cathryn Coale began visiting Casper's grade schools to talk about library programs, tell stories, and distribute library cards to the children. Davis attributed the increased attendance at story hour and the "enormous increase" in the use of children's books at the library to these visits. Davis reported that the children's room circulated nearly 9,000 more books in 1928 than in 1927.

Encouraging children to use the library, however, had one challenging aspect – dealing with unruly youngsters. Place reported to the Library Board on April 10, 1911, that parents were being advised "to either control their children or to keep them away from the library." This problem would persist throughout the years.

Outreach to the Community

Despite the problem of unruly children, the second program stimulated by Natrona County's boom-era growth was an outreach program that Rodgers created in the early 1920s to make the children's collections available to outlying schools. While there is no evidence to suggest that Rodgers modeled this outreach service after a traveling library that the Midwest Refining Company created for its oilfield camps, there is an intriguing parallel between the Midwest idea and Rodgers's program.

A 1921 issue of the magazine *Midwest Review* discusses the Midwest traveling library concept by explaining that the company's industrial-relations department constructed seven "strong, well made" boxes to house books. The department then filled each box with fifty items: children's books, biographies, history, travel, and geology, with special emphasis on the petroleum industry. These books would travel to the Midwest Refining Company's camps at Salt Creek (Home Camp), Osage, Elk Basin, Salt Creek (Gas Plant), Teapot Station, Big Muddy, and Grass Creek. At each of these camps, the company clerk circulated the books to the camp's residents. After two months the crates would be rotated to another camp. Then, at the end of the fourteen-month rotation, the books would be replaced by a new set of books.

The public library's outreach program was similar to the Midwest idea. Mokler recorded in his *History of Natrona County* that in 1921 the library sent books to schools in places such as "Salt Creek, Kasoming, Ohio Camp, Poison Spider, Alcova and other schools in the county." The library's 1928 annual report elaborated on the practice by commenting that outlying schools such as McKinley, Lincoln, Willard, Mills, Mountain View, and "all the rural schools" received between 50 and 125 books and that these books were exchanged every two months. Also, teachers in Casper's schools were encouraged to borrow "collections of ten books at a time as class room libraries." The report stated that the goal of this outreach program was to allow "the children living too far from the central library" to check out books for reading at home.

Growing populations and the need to expand library services are not the only enduring concerns of county librarians. One challenge that seems always to demand a library's resources and often tests a librarian's patience is lost, stolen, or mutilated books and other materials. The same January 1925 news article that reported the library's growing demand for nonfiction books also commented on a significant problem that the library was facing as its usage increased: "The loss of many valuable books continues to distress [the library staff] greatly.... [We have] been obliged to take many valuable reference books from the open shelves entirely for safe-keeping." The loss of library materials is a problem that seems to defy perfect solutions, as attested by the fact that the Natrona County Public Library continues to explore ways of dealing with it.

Building maintenance, particularly the ongoing need for roof repairs, also demanded the library's attention. In November 1911, for example, the library spent $27 to repair the new roof. In 1912, the roof needed additional repairs. Again, in 1926, the library paid a company $200 to repair the roof. Repair, remodeling, and restoration of the library building would become a persistent requirement over the years.

Building Expansion

Beyond simple maintenance and repair, however, by the early 1920s Rodgers faced a much more pressing need: the necessity of dealing with congestion caused by the expansion of the library's collections, additional staff members, and increased numbers of visitors. In 1922, Library Board member Charles H. Townsend suggested to the County Commissioners that they might soon need to enlarge the library building. "At the present time," he announced, "this library has very comfortable quarters, although it is somewhat limited in space for the rapidly growing community." He concluded, "On account of the increased patronage of the library, it will be but a short time until the building must be enlarged."

This strong statement emphasized the value of the library to the county by the mid-1920s. A brief, undated manuscript titled "Natrona County Library History" succinctly explained the positive nature of the library's growing pains: "Fourteen years after the official establishment of the Natrona County Public Library, the [library's governing] association had gotten firmly established in the community and the demands made upon it had brought about the time for expansion." Of all of the challenges the library has faced historically – leaky roofs, unruly children, overcrowding – the need to expand its facilities has been the most persistent concern.

At the June 6, 1924, Board meeting, "Mrs. Rodgers reported the library [was] being used freely by the public. The demands being such that the room was inadequate to give good service." The Trustees took action before the end of the year. At the December 1, 1924, Board meeting, Billy Johnson made the motion to contact Leon C. Goodrich, a local architect and partner with the firm of Dubois & Goodrich, to confer with the Trustees on creating a plan to alleviate the library's overcrowding. In January 1925, Goodrich presented such a plan to the Trustees, who in turn instructed him to request bids for construction. The architect held a meeting of prospective contractors in his office on February 25, 1925.

In 1925, Casper architect Leon Goodrich designed an addition perfectly fitted to the original Carnegie-style library building.
Detail from 1956 photo of Kimball Coffee Club members courtesy Casper College Western History Center, David Memorial Collection.

Goodrich's plans called for an addition to be attached to the 1910 Carnegie library building. The architect preserved and enhanced the Carnegie Classic architectural style by complementing the features of the old building and by adding an attractive frieze-covered entrance to the new structure. In his plans, Goodrich made it very clear that the construction work was to mirror the existing building. The specifications supported this intent: "Cornice and jamb quoins, sills and all caps are to be made of stone to match old work"; "Build cornice, frieze and architrave mould on new part similar to old cornice in all respects"; "New columns, caps, coping and bases are to be made of similar stone." Decades later, whenever this author viewed the Carnegie library and its addition, he never realized that he was looking at the result of two separate periods of construction. It came as a pleasant but startling surprise in 2005 when the author learned from architectural drawings that the building he had always thought to be a single piece of construction was in reality two separate structures.

The successful bidder for the construction project was the Casper firm of Colby & Rognstad that offered to do the work for $27,300. Funds used for the building included $21,500 of unspent library appropriations that had accumulated over the previous fifteen years. The County Commissioners allowed the library to keep any unspent portion of its annual budget each year to invest in interest-bearing certificates of deposit so that the funds would be available to the library for future expenditures such as a construction project. Board Chairman Townsend explained this at a meeting of Casper's Board of Realtors in May 1925. He did this to counter the grumblings of some "chronic knockers" who claimed the building would cost the taxpayers $40,000.

This view of the north and west facades of the Carnegie library shows the seamless design of the 1925 addition.
Undated photo by Beach's Studio courtesy Casper College Western History Center, Ruth Scott Hocker Collection.

New Features, Special Collections

When completed in late 1925, the new library facility featured an entrance on Durbin Street, a second set of stacks, a librarian's office, a cataloging room, and a new children's room that included "a big fireplace, well selected pictures and blooming plants," and room for 3,000 books. In addition, the 1925 structure had a full basement that included a large assembly room, separate men's and women's restrooms, and a storage room.

Given the spaciousness of their new facility, the Board of Trustees offered the Natrona County Historical Association space to establish a permanent museum in the library's old Club Room. The Historical Association accepted the offer, and the Library Board members instructed Goodrich to design a set of glass display cases. When finished, these cases cost $1,500. In February 1926, the *Casper Daily Tribune* reported the completion of the new museum and mentioned that one of the items on display was a "mummified Indian Chief Skeleton with his regalia and trappings." A. N. Keith of Kaycee, Wyoming, gave this skeleton to the museum on a long-term loan.

Also of historical note, the library had long been collecting books for a Wyoming history collection. The *Casper Daily Tribune* noted on January 9, 1927, that the library's collection of "valuable Americana, particularly books relating to the early history of Wyoming" had outgrown its allotted space, so the librarian was planning to have a locked case built in the reading room. The library's 1929 annual report emphasized the growth and importance of this collection, declaring, "A large number of books have been added to the Wyoming collection, which now numbers 393 volumes, many of them rare and out of print."

Another specialized collection relevant to Natrona County and its oil-related economic growth was that of various publications put out by the United States Geological Survey (USGS).

By 1925, the library had more than 700 items in its USGS collection. In July 1929, Wyoming's United States Senator John Kendrick announced that the Natrona County Public Library would become a depository for government documents, the first Wyoming public library to be so selected. According to the 1929 annual report, "The library is now receiving the new issues, as published, of 67 series, including the publications of the Geological Survey and the Bureau of Mines."

The Unwritten Catalog

In 1927, while still actively engaged as the county's Head Librarian, Effie Rodgers became ill and died. Board member Johnson wrote in a four-page manuscript titled "Natrona County Library Notes" that Rodgers "knew the location

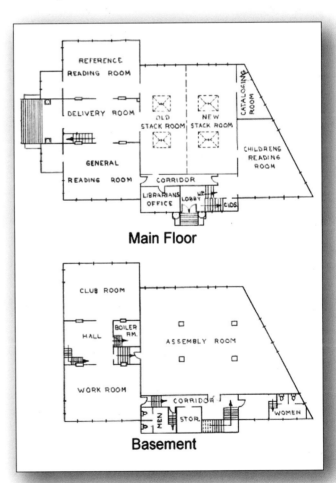

The library design as revised in 1925 featured a special children's department and a large meeting room. Floor plan from NCPL files.

of every item on the [library's] shelves" and that she "had no difficulty in furnishing patrons with any information needed." He observed, however, that her death presented the library with a special challenge because, with her passing, "our Catalogue also 'passed away.'" In other words, the library had no effective set of card catalog drawers. Rodgers simply relied on memory to locate library materials for visitors. Assistant librarian Elva Randa became the acting librarian until the Trustees could hire a new librarian.

As they began a search for Rodgers's replacement, the Trustees made it a priority to find a librarian with cataloging experience. They accomplished this when they hired, apparently sight-unseen, Eleanor Davis, who had received library training at the University of Washington, where she worked for one year as an assistant cataloger. In addition, Davis had one year of reference experience at the Minneapolis Public Library and five years at the Oregon State Library and a high school library in Portland, Oregon. Before traveling to Casper to begin her work as the Head Librarian, Davis wrote to the Library Board, "Would you please write me all the pleasant particulars about your library that I may have a better idea of what I am going to? I expect to arrive in Casper on the early morning train Monday, April Second, via Cheyenne."

Upon beginning her work, Davis hired Ellen MacGregor to work with the library's typist, Elnora Barbee, on "recataloging the library." Davis stated in the 1928 annual report, "By December 31, 5,517 books for adults and 4,003 children's books have been cataloged, a total of 9,520." Davis continued, "Of this total, 5,302 were new books added during the year, while 4,218 were recataloged. About 18,000 volumes remain to be recataloged." In her 1929 annual report, Davis closed out this project by announcing, "The recataloging of the library, begun in June 1928, was completed in July 1929."

Summary

By the end of the 1920s, the Natrona County Public Library had become a valuable and well-used institution to the people of the county. Its collections had grown from the 850 books housed in the original Carnegie library to a collection of 29,900 books and 100 magazine subscriptions. Its staff had increased from one librarian in 1910 to a librarian, a children's librarian, a circulation assistant, a custodian, and a half-time assistant to do shelving and book repair in 1930. Likewise, the librarian's salary had increased, from $50 per month in 1910 to $200 per month in 1929. The number of people with library cards rose from 200 in 1910 to 5,400 in 1929. Circulation numbers increased dramatically, from either 1,000 books (Mokler) or 2,800 (Board minutes) in 1911 to 177,500 by the end of 1929. In similar fashion, the library budget had increased from less than $2,000 in 1910 to $33,200 in 1929.

The Natrona County Public Library underwent significant physical alterations during its first twenty years. The most apparent change was the 1925 addition to the original Carnegie library. The new building doubled the space available for shelves, reading rooms, meeting rooms, and offices. Library employees added services to meet the growing demands. These new services included children's story hours, books to outlying schools within the county, a museum, and enhanced Wyoming history, federal document, and reference collections.

By the end of the 1920s, the Natrona County Public Library had become so well organized and so firmly established that there was no doubt as to the value it offered to patrons. Given the building's expansion, the growth in collections, the increases in staff and use of the facility, the library stood on firm enough ground in 1929 to weather the forthcoming years of the Great Depression.

Chapter Three: Hard Times Descend

1929-1945

There is not such a cradle of democracy upon the earth as the Free Public Library, this republic of letters, where neither rank, office, nor wealth receive the slightest consideration.

Andrew Carnegie

Wall Street may have crashed in 1929, but hard times began creeping across the country, including Natrona County, years before that. As early as January 1925, the *Casper Daily Tribune* quoted Librarian Effie Rodgers as saying, "Neither business depression nor inclement weather affect our work in any marked degree." A *Denver Post* article of November 25, 1951, recalled, "Crude oil prices were slashed three times in 1927." Reporting on conditions in Wyoming, the newspaper continued, "You could rent an empty store or house in Casper surprisingly cheap." By 1929, the price of oil had plunged to historic lows. "Hell," one longtime oilfield roustabout declared, "we'd already been depressed for quite awhile." And the local economy would suffer for years to come.

By 1930, unemployed workers were flocking to Casper; by 1934, 700 destitute families lived in the city. By 1936, the County Commissioners were forced to reduce spending by laying off four deputy sheriffs, three jailers, the food inspector, and the entire county highway department. Natrona County assessment values illustrate the distressing situation. In 1929, the county reported a valuation of $87.3 million, but in 1930 the figure had dropped to $60.7 million. By the mid-1930s, the figure was $40 million. In 1945, the county cited a valuation of only $31.3 million.

In 1937, the City of Casper followed the county's example of belt-tightening by laying off forty-seven employees. The Casper population shrank dramatically. In annual reports to the Wyoming State Library, Natrona County's librarians cited grim figures. In 1929, the city's population was 35,100, but by the end of 1930, it had declined to 24,000. By 1940, as the war in Europe began to stimulate the nation's economic recovery, Casper had only 20,000 residents.

However, the Natrona County Public Library did not suffer statistically in the first two years of the Depression. While the library budget was $33,200 in 1929, it actually increased to $34,500 in 1930 before dropping to $30,700 in 1931 and then plummeting to barely $18,300 by 1935. Reflecting the county's slow economic recovery, the library's budget did not rise much above $19,000 until several years after the Second World War.

During that period, two of the Library Board of Trustees' three members, Billy Johnson and Carl F. Shumaker, provided stability and leadership throughout some of the most trying times

Spotlight: 1930
Natrona County Population: 24,300
Casper Population: 16,600

Natrona County Public Library Facts
Head Librarian: Eleanor Davis
Library Collection: 35,800
Circulation: 224,200
Budget: $34,500
Board Members: Philip. K. Edwards,
    J. W. "Billy" Johnson, Carl F. Shumaker

in the library's long history. The County Commissioners appointed Johnson to the Board in 1918 to replace early member John E. Schulte (1909-1918), and subsequent Commissioners continued to reappoint Johnson until he retired in 1965. Shumaker, Vice-President of Wyoming National Bank, also served as a Trustee for the entire period of the Great Depression and the Second World War. Appointed in 1927, he remained on the Board until 1945.

During the early years of the Great Depression, Eleanor Davis guided the library with dedication and focus. Her accomplishments as Head Librarian demonstrated an unshakable commitment to her profession and to the Natrona County Public Library. Billy Johnson once commented that Davis was a "bundle of energy" whose only trait that might be viewed as a shortcoming was an intensity that seemed never to allow her to sit down and visit with people. But she got work done.

Billy Johnson served on the NCPL Board of Trustees for forty-seven years, longer than any other Board member.
Photo courtesy of Billy Johnson's family.

A Branch at Midwest

One of the crowning achievements of Davis's tenure was the establishment of a branch library in Midwest, Wyoming. At the March 1929 Library Board meeting, just months before the stock market crash that October, the Trustees reviewed a petition from Midwest residents requesting a branch library. Five months later, the Board reported that the County Commissioners had appropriated $3,000 for a Midwest Branch Library. On February 28, 1930, Library Board President Shumaker co-signed, with Midwest Refining Company official R. S. Ellison, an agreement detailing the arrangements for the operation of the Midwest Branch Library.

In the agreement, the Midwest Refining Company provided a location for the library: "That certain room…in the rear or furthermost west room on the second floor of that certain two story frame building known as Midwest Refining Company No. 567, situated at the corner of Ellison Avenue and Wilson Street, in the oilfield camp of Midwest." The agreement stated that the Natrona County Public Library was responsible for furnishing books, magazines, supplies, and a librarian's salary. The Midwest Refining Company agreed to provide shelving for 4,000 books, tables and chairs to accommodate up to twenty-five readers, heat, lights, ordinary repairs, and janitorial services.

Showing great satisfaction with this turn of events, Davis wrote in her 1930 annual report, "The outstanding event of the year was the opening on March 24, 1930, of the Midwest Branch Library to serve the people of the oilfield. An appropriation to start this branch, made by the County Commissioners at their annual meeting of 1929, became available in January 1930." She continued, "A large and attractive room was provided, shelved and furnished by the Midwest Refining Company, and the library opened in March with approximately 1,500 books on its shelves." Interestingly, 1,500 books was approximately 40 percent more books than the county library's main location in Casper possessed when it opened on May 21, 1910.

Ella Chandler was the first employee in charge of the Midwest Branch. By the end of 1930, the Midwest Branch had signed up 1,400 borrowers and circulated 28,800 books. Circulation increased to 41,400 in 1934.

In 1935, however, the Midwest Branch Library began to experience the negative effects of the Great Depression. The Natrona County Public Library's 1935 annual report stated that use of the Midwest Branch had slowed "due to the decrease of population in the oil field." The 1940 annual report noted that the branch's circulation statistics were not "up to par" as a result of "the depletion of borrowers in the camps." In 1945, borrowers checked out only 7,000 books, a scant one-sixth of the number circulated in 1934.

Rural Library Stations and Outreach

In 1928, the library's annual report briefly and somewhat cryptically mentioned the existence of two library stations within the county. The 1941 annual report referred to one station with a circulation of 1,800 books for that year. The 1944 report mentioned a station at Powder River, Wyoming. The Board of Trustees' minutes for March 14, 1945, noted that the Powder River station was closed because the library could not find a replacement for the woman who managed the small operation.

While there are no descriptions of how these stations functioned or how large they were, it is reasonable to assume that they were small and perhaps located in an out-of-the-way place in a rural community's general store. Theodore Jones's work *Carnegie Libraries Across America* describes just such a station: a "public book collection in the millinery section of [Olive Griffin's] family's store in Corydon, Indiana." The note accompanies a photograph showing two small bookshelves stocked with approximately twenty-five volumes.

Eleanor Davis guided the library through the darkest years of the Great Depression. After leaving Casper, Davis held several other library posts. She is shown here as a member of the Douglas County (Oregon) library staff, 25 years after leaving NCPL.
Published January 26, 1962 in the News-Review, *Roseburg Oregon. Reprinted with permission.*

Such outreach efforts began in the 1920s and flourished in the 1930s and 1940s. One means of conducting outreach was to send books to outlying schools. The library's 1931 annual report announced, "Books have been sent to the rural schools of the county and to an increasing number of individual rural borrowers." In 1936, the library's annual report elaborated on the practice of serving residents beyond the confines of the library itself. "As in former years," the report stated, "books have been sent to all rural schools. Within the city, classroom libraries have been sent to all rooms in four schools located farthest from the library, and also to a large number of rooms in nearer schools." This sharing of books reflected the Midwest Refining Company's traveling libraries and predated the use of bookmobiles. These programs illustrate not only the desire of people to make use of public library resources, but also the ingenuity and willingness of librarians to accommodate patrons living in distant locations.

In 1937, children gathered around the juvenile department Christmas tree to read.
Photo from NCPL files.

Programs for Children

Children's programs served an outreach function of the Natrona County Public Library while entertaining and educating people in the county. Through the use of story hour, displays, and visits to public schools, the library continued to reach out to young people during the 1930s and 1940s.

In 1931, Head Librarian Eleanor Davis reported, "Story hour has been held weekly during the year by the children's librarian [Cathryn Coale]." Book Week was one way of engaging the county's youth. This event, Davis said, "was celebrated by the display of a large number of new books for children, and a lavish display of posters made by the Girl Scouts of the city." In 1932, Book Week posters and displays featured "lists of books about children in other lands" and that these lists were mimeographed at the high school for the library and then "distributed to all

grade school teachers in Casper and through the county to aid them in making more use of the [library's] junior room." In addition, Coale invited each grade-school class to visit the library during the autumn of 1932. During these visits, she talked about the library, gave tours, and encouraged students to use the library.

Coale left the library and Casper in 1933 to marry, at which point story hour was discontinued for a time. Before the end of the year, however, Margaret Brown replaced Coale and soon immersed herself in working with the area's young people. For Book Week in November 1934, she had children from the fourth through seventh grades send her lists of their favorite hobbies. Learning that the most widespread hobbies included pets, sports, stamp and rock collecting, handicrafts, and drawing, she prepared lists of books on these and related subjects and then

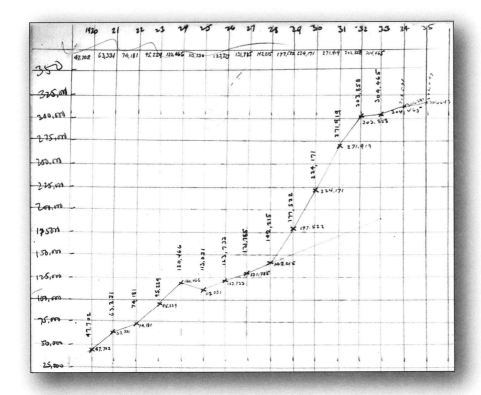

This hand-drawn graph contained in Eleanor Davis's 1935 annual report shows how the library's circulation growth began to taper off in the early 1930s before actually showing a decrease in 1936. The number of books circulated, as well as the number of borrowers, continued to decline into the 1940s, corresponding with the county's decreasing population.
Illustration from NCPL files.

sent her lists to the children who had noted their interests. After this, she held a hobby show with the help of Casper's Girl Scouts and Boy Scouts and took the results of this show to downtown stores where display windows "were filled with articles representing various hobbies and the books about them." She then created book displays at the library, efforts that led to "a surprising demand for books on a wide range of subjects."

Ups and Downs

Initially, the nation's economic woes seemed not to affect the public library. The number of registered patrons at the main library increased from 7,900 in 1929, to 14,700 in 1935. Likewise, the number of books borrowed each year, including books circulated throughout outlying schools, increased from 177,500 in 1929, to 306,600 in 1935.

Then came a reversal of fortunes. As with the Midwest Branch, the county's main library in Casper began to feel the pinch of difficult times. In her 1936 annual report, Head Librarian Eleanor Davis noted, "For the first time since 1926, the

library has failed to show an increased circulation over the previous year." The number of borrowers decreased as well. At first the decline was slow, but it remained steady and then fell sharply to a low of 8,600 registered patrons in 1945.

The addition of new books, magazines, and newspapers also suffered during the 1930s. At the end of 1933, Davis wrote, "Because of lower appropriation, it was found necessary to reduce the book budget by almost half. As a result, fewer books have been purchased during 1933 than during any recent year." However, this situation seems to have been temporary. Statistics show a long-term increase in book collections, suggesting an effective and aggressive acquisitions program through the Great Depression and the Second World War. In 1929, for example, the library had 29,900 books. The collection increased to 65,400 by the end of 1945.

A seemingly unending problem intensified in the 1930s – the loss of books through theft, vandalism, and mutilation. On January 9, 1933, Board members heard Davis vent her frustration at the serious nature of the book thefts and the library being overrun by an "undesirable element," consisting largely of high school students, vandalizing the institution's books. The following day Davis gave Board President Carl Shumaker a letter detailing her concerns. "There has recently been an increase in theft and vandalism in the library," she wrote. "Books are being stolen and others mutilated to an alarming extent. Pages, and in some cases whole chapters and sections of books have been cut or torn out, poems torn from anthologies, and illustrations cut out and torn from magazines and books."

Davis's letter continued, "Many of our most valuable books, including encyclopedias, art books and beautifully illustrated editions have been mutilated." She then fixed on the cause: "We believe that a considerable part of this vandalism is directly traceable to high school and junior high school students who are asked by their teachers to find illustrations for their note books." To show the depths of her feelings regarding this situation, Davis wrote, "In the public library it is impossible to check this evil." She surmised, "There may be a question as to whether this activity of cutting out pictures and pasting them in note books is essential to the intellectual development of high school students."

For most of the years between 1929 and 1945, the library was open from 1:00 p.m. to 9:00 p.m., Monday through Saturday. For a time at the beginning of the Great Depression, the library was open on Sundays. During the August 21, 1935, Board meeting, Davis reported that the library had lost large numbers of books during recent years because of theft. The Trustees concluded that one way of "dealing with this evil" was to close the library on Sundays.

The library's loss of books did not end there. In the 1935 annual report, Davis again articulated her concerns over lost items. In a mood as glum as the Depression itself, she noted that library staff members had completed an inventory during the year. As a result, she learned that between 1928 and 1935, the library had lost 600 books to 360 borrowers who had moved out of the county without returning their items. Then she moved on to worse news, "Theft of books constitutes a much more serious problem." Davis continued, "During the same seven year period, 2,612 books have been taken from the shelves without being charged." She calculated that this was 5 percent of the library's entire collection. "Among the fiction," she stated, "Popular fiction, Western stories in particular, showed the greatest loss." Again, she termed the loss of books "this evil," and concluded her report by comparing Casper's borrowers to those in Midwest: "The Midwest Branch, established in 1930, showed a loss of only slightly over 1%." Frustrated as she was by this situation, her concerns addressed a problem that remains eternal to libraries.

Retrieving overdue books was also problematic for the library. As Davis noted in 1935, overdue materials had a cumulative impact on the library. In 1937, the Library Board approved hiring a person at twenty-five cents per hour to pursue those patrons who had failed to return library books. Jerry Hand (later to become an attorney, whose wife, Agnes, served on the Library Board from 1987 to 1993) agreed to retrieve overdue materials for the library during the Great Depression. Hand used his bicycle for the job. After wrapping his newspaper bags over the handlebars of the bike, he reported to the library to obtain data cards on patrons who had overdue books. Then he rode to their homes. His reimbursement for this work was 50 percent of the amount of money he collected as late fees on the books he brought back.

Library Grounds

In addition to the issue of lost and stolen books, the library faced larger challenges. One of these was the threat of losing the library's land. In 1935, the County Commissioners leased a forty-foot strip of the library's lawn to Oscar

August 17, 1933

Board of Trustees
Natrona County Library
Casper Wyo.

Gentlemen:

This is our bid for painting work.

We will do the work as initally outlined in your specification for the sum of $144.00 - One hundred and forty four dollars.

Good work will be done, and care used so that articles in the rooms will not be spattered.

Very truly yours

This 1933 bid for painting library interiors displays the National Recovery Act stamp. Local businesses participated in efforts to survive and revive the national economy. Bid letter from NCPL files.

Whitlock for commercial purposes. Concerned with this event, the Library Board voted to let the Commissioners know that their action might be unwise because the Carey family of Cheyenne, Wyoming, had given their land to Natrona County in the hope that it be used for a library. This threat of the loss of land persisted to the extent that longtime Library Trustee Billy Johnson noted, "One of our biggest problems for a good many years was to retain possession of the East Portion of the lot which was vacant until… later used for our [1952 addition]." He added, "Different individuals were constantly trying to get possession of portions of it to 'tie into' portions of railroad land to the [library's] rear."

Maintenance and Renovations

Another continual challenge for the employees and Trustees of the county library was building maintenance. According to the 1930 annual report, "Several improvements have been made in the appearance of the building. During the summer the walls were kalsomined [the application of a white or tinted wash used mainly on plaster surfaces], the interior woodwork varnished, and the exterior woodwork painted." In addition to this facelift, the report stated, "Transoms were added to the stack-room windows, new shelving built for magazines, a new case for bound newspapers, new files at the front desk, and new chairs purchased for the large club-room."

In 1933, library officials continued to ensure that the Carnegie building and its addition remained in good shape. This time the Board of Trustees advertised for bids to paint and use kalsomine on water-damaged parts of the ceiling, floors, and walls in the reference, stacks, and hallway rooms on the main level, as well as in some areas of the large and small club rooms and the front hall in the basement. Five local firms bid on the work: E. G. Ericksen & Sons, John Jourgensen Paints, L. D. Leisinger, M. R. Davis, and Redwine Building Company. Redwine submitted the low bid of fifty-eight dollars to do the painting and kalsomine work on the walls and ceiling and twelve dollars to paint the floors.

The Ericksen and Jourgensen bids illustrated the effects of the Depression on local business and politics. The Ericksen bid was submitted on recycled paper, typed on the back of a Chamber of Commerce advertisement titled "Wyoming: The Wonder State; Unique In Its Agricultural, Industrial and Recreational Advantages." The Jourgensen bid was a two-page submission with a National Recovery Act sticker on each page. The National Recovery Act stamp was a vivid reflection of the Great Depression and President Franklin Delano Roosevelt's New Deal program. Sidewalks, buildings, parks, and other facilities in Natrona County were created with New Deal funds, and the library was able to employ one worker, Emma Earle, with Works Progress Administration money.

Once again, in 1940, library administrators sought to renovate the interior of the Casper structure. Work on the building would include new linoleum, chairs for the children's area, a new circulation desk, and curtains for the staff room. The annual report, noting a decrease in the number of books being checked out that year, announced, "The drop in total circulation is due to the fact that the library was closed for almost eight weeks for remodeling." The librarian need not have apologized for the inconvenience, however, because circulation statistics indicate that 1940 simply followed a trend toward fewer

books being checked out. The total in 1940 was 242,400 (including 24,800 at the Midwest Branch) but dropped to 225,700 in 1942 (21,900 for Midwest) and 131,600 in 1945 (7,000 for Midwest).

Another maintenance concern throughout the 1930s was roof repair. Almost from the time the original Carnegie library was constructed, leaks in the roof plagued the librarian and the Board of Trustees. Board minutes from June 1930, May 1932, July 1933, June 1939, September 1939, and August 1943 reflected an ongoing struggle to keep the library's roof in good shape. At its Board meeting on August 6, 1943, the Board selected the Rohlff Lumber Company, which had previously fixed the library's roof, to again "see to the care of the roofing."

Carnegie and the Depression

One pleasant echo of the library's origin occurred in 1935 when the Carnegie Foundation sent a framed copy of Francis Luis Mora's painted portrait of Carnegie to all libraries that had been constructed with Carnegie money. Although the fate of the painting is unknown, a news clipping circa 1955 commented on the significance of the gift: "Casper's [Carnegie] portrait reproduction framed for permanent keeping when presented, as were all of the others, still hangs in the old Carnegie building."

Visitors to the Natrona County Public Library during the Great Depression had special reason to appreciate Carnegie's 1906 financial gift to Casper. In the 1930s, the library offered county residents a safe and rewarding place to spend their time. In her 1932 annual report, Eleanor Davis eloquently described the value of the library to its patrons: "Unemployment, here as elsewhere, is sending readers to the library with a consequent increase in the demand for books on such technical and professional subjects as woodworking, machine shop practice, lathes, civil service examinations, homestead laws, salesmanship, advertising, diesel engines, prospecting and mining."

PORTRAIT IN OLD SECTION: The portrait of Andrew Carnegie, which has an honored place in the old section of the Natrona County Public Library, is a reproduction of an original painted by Luis Mora. As a part of the Andrew Carnegie centennial celebration in 1935, the Carnegie Corp. of New York presented copies of the portrait to all Carnegie libraries in the United States and the British Dominions and colonies. The doorway leads to the newer section of the library—(Tribune-Star Photo).

Herein lies one of the greatest values of a free public library – providing a wide variety of educational books to the public. Carnegie, a man who valued hard work and the acquisition of knowledge in the pursuit of personal betterment, clearly saw this crucial characteristic of a public library. Those who used the Natrona County Public Library during the Depression also saw its value. Davis sensed this. In 1934, she wrote, "A change to more serious reading is indicated by the fact that 6,000 fewer volumes of fiction were borrowed by adults in 1934 than in 1933." She continued, "A growing demand is noticed for information books, especially scientific and technical books including such subjects as geology, mineralogy, engineering, mining, surveying, mathematics, land and soils, irrigation." She added, "There has also been a greatly increased demand for Wyoming and western history."

The library's activities during these dark years emphasized an attempt to meet the practical needs of county residents. The display case at the library's main entrance offered glimpses into the institution's diverse collections. In 1931, for example, the library displayed twenty-eight groups of books, among which were items on mining, mineralogy, and geology recommended by the Wyoming state geologist. Accompanying the display of books were "posters and

Genevra Brock, a Wyoming native, was Natrona County's Head Librarian for six years. Photo from NCPL files.

annotated lists sometimes with a brief article" that the local newspaper published.

In addition, the library enlarged its special collections, which included a Wyoming collection and a section for federal documents. Davis reported during the first months of the Great Depression, "A large number of books have been added to the Wyoming collection, which now number 393 volumes, many of them rare and out of print." Of the federal document collection, Davis reported in 1930, "The government documents, which the library has received since it became a depository in 1929, have been [cataloged]. The publications of the U.S. Geological Survey, Bureau of Mines, Department of Agriculture, Bureau of Education, Children's Bureau and other government departments are included." These unique collections increased the library's usefulness to Depression-era readers.

Staff Changes

In September 1937, Eleanor Davis resigned her position at the Natrona County Public Library to take a library job in another city. She had guided the county's library through most of the worst years of the Depression. Board member Billy Johnson once remarked that she had "a big job to do" at the county library. The nation's economic crisis also had affected her personally. In 1929, her salary was $2,400 annually. In 1932, the Board decreased it by 10 percent. In 1934 it was $2,200. Yet she did her job and, as Johnson noted, "As her work was practically finished with our library it was not long until she was offered a place in a larger city."

Genevra Brock replaced Davis before the end of September 1937. She was the sister of longtime Casper resident and real estate and insurance agent Clarence Brock. Originally from Johnson County, Wyoming, Brock had done summer training in library work at the University of Wyoming. From 1921 to 1923, she served as the Wyoming State Librarian. While at the Natrona County

Public Library, she also served as an officer in the Wyoming Library Association and was elected as the Vice-President/President-Elect in 1942.

Brock's tenure at the Natrona County Public Library was marked by a deepening national economic depression and the Second World War, both of which affected the library's operations negatively. Although she was able to retain her eight library employees and to procure a fairly steady budget each year (averaging $17,000), during her tenure there was a decrease in both the number of library cards held by county residents and the number of books checked out. From 1937 to 1943, the number of people who held library cards diminished by nearly 40 percent, dropping from around 15,300 to just over 9,500. The number of books checked out plummeted from approximately 265,000 to less than 150,000. In 1943, Brock married, resigned her position at the library, and moved to Florida.

When Brock left the library, Margaret Burke took her place. Born in Nebraska, Burke earned a master's degree from the University of Colorado at Boulder. In 1927, she moved to Casper to care for her mother, then left to study library

Spotlight: 1940
Natrona County Population: 23,900
Casper Population: 20,000

Natrona County Public Library Facts
Head Librarian: Genevra Brock
Library Collection: 63,100
Circulation: 242,400
Budget: $21,300
Board Members: J. W. "Billy" Johnson, Nell Kimball, Carl F. Shumaker

science at the University of Illinois. Upon Burke's return to Casper, Brock hired her as the assistant librarian. As Head Librarian after Brock's departure, Burke presided over more than a decade of increased use and expanded physical facilities.

The number of staff remained fairly constant between 1929 and 1945. Positions included a head librarian, an assistant, a children's librarian, a branch librarian, two assistants to do clerical work and shelving, a janitor, and one or more other part-time workers. Despite the decreased library budget, the Board of Trustees provided for

After her promotion to Head Librarian, Margaret Burke fought for funding for another addition to the library. Photo from NCPL files.

1942

The library staff, including Margaret Burke (third from right), gathered for this photo in 1942. Photo from NCPL files.

library employees as well as it could. Sporadically from the mid-1930s onward, each full-time staff member received a Christmas bonus of five dollars. In 1940, the Trustees also gave two dollars and fifty cents to each part-time employee. The Library Board's minutes from March 14, 1945, noted that library employees would be granted a five-dollar increase in their monthly wages.

On October 8, 1945, the Library Board held its regular monthly meeting. After matters of business were conducted, Board Secretary Billy Johnson recorded the gist of a conversation among the Board members: "There was a lengthy discussion on the feasibility and need of the construction of a wing to the present library building." The Board then instructed Burke to contact various library-related organizations, such as the American Library Association, the Library Bureau, and supplier Gaylord Brothers, as well as local architect Leon

C. Goodrich. Johnson and his colleagues, Carl Shumaker and Thomas Spears (a Board member from 1943 until his death in 1947), wanted to consider possible floor plans for an expanded library.

Summary

By 1945, the Natrona County Public Library had weathered fifteen years of economic depression and global war. Despite these hard times, the library grew in book collections, staff, and building size to better serve residents throughout the county. At the October 8, 1945, meeting, the library leaders began to lay the groundwork for expanded service and facilities that would carry the library forward into the 1950s and 1960s. By this time, life had improved in Casper and Natrona County, and library officials were determined that the library would continue to improve with the county it served.

Chapter Four: Renewed Growth

1945-1969

Libraries are places where communities can learn, live and grow.

Carolyn Crawford Bentzen, Daughter of Board Member James G. Crawford

Prosperity returned to Natrona County soon after the end of the Second World War despite nationwide inflation and labor unrest, shortages of such commodities as meat, sugar, and other everyday items, and a housing shortage in Casper. The county population increased continually from a prewar figure of 23,900 to approximately 43,000 in 1969. The county's assessed valuation improved from $31.3 million in 1946 to $144.1 million in 1969. Oil production surged again, and by the end of the 1940s, Casper had regained its regional status as Oil Capital of the Rockies. At the same time, Natrona County had the highest property values in Wyoming. Within a decade, residents of the county approved a $1 million bond to expand the county's hospital, a $350,000 bond to build a new terminal at the county airport at the former Casper Army Air Base, and $2.3 million to construct the first campus building at Casper College.

For the Natrona County Public Library, however, the return of the county's prosperity did not mean immediate improvement in budgets, patronage, or circulation. For much of the next twenty-five years, the library experienced slow, often halting growth that reflected neither a decline in the library's value to the community nor the fast-paced growth of boom times. The library budget was an example of this growth pattern. In 1946, the county provided the library with $19,100. In 1949, the sum was increased to

$24,100. The budget was decreased again, but in 1953 it reached a historic high of $85,600. Thereafter, the library budget fluctuated, hovering around $75,000 until 1964, when it rose to $93,200. In 1969, it stood at $151,500. Circulation statistics suggest the same vacillations. In 1946, 131,600 items were borrowed from the library. This figure more than doubled by 1964, when it reached a twenty-five-year high of 276,400. Yet even this figure pales in comparison to the 1935 circulation record of 306,600.

Margaret Burke was a champion of outreach programs encouraging children to read. Photo from NCPL files circa 1952.

The up-and-down nature of the budget and circulation figures hides a genuine vitality that the library experienced between 1946 and 1969. During this time, the library's success was due in large part to Head Librarians Margaret Burke (1943-1957) and LaFrances McCoy Sullivan (1957-1969).

Burke was described by colleague Janice Chamberlain as a steadfast worker who was immensely "formidable" with her long dresses and cane, but who "was always very kind." Burke was extremely active in community affairs. A member of St. Anthony's Roman Catholic Church, she was in the Altar and Rosary Society and the Aquinas Club. She was also a member of the American Association of University Women and the Professional Women's Club of Casper and, for several terms, was President of the Wyoming Library Association. Reaching out beyond the library, she was able to apply her activism to library causes. In 1955, she assisted in a reading program created by the local school district's primary-education coordinator, Flo Rogers.

Rogers was known as "The Bookworm Lady." She encouraged the county's second- and third-grade students to become more interested in reading. Rogers developed an incentive program that encompassed the public library and grade schools at Casper, Midwest, Alcova, Poison Spider, and Devil's Gate. Rogers

took all of her Bookworm students to the library four times annually. The program concluded with a ceremony to reward those who had read the requisite number of books. To second-grade achievers, Rogers gave a ceramic bookworm. Third-graders received a ceramic candle in a holder. All participants received bookworm pins.

In addition to ensuring the library participated in the Bookworm program, Burke cooperated with the school district in the summers of 1956 and 1957 to create the county's first bookmobile. This vehicle was a secondhand grocery delivery truck that the school district converted into a bookmobile so that schools and the library could continue the Bookworm program through the summer months. The school district paid a high school girl, Patricia Howard, to drive the old grocery truck while the public library stocked the truck with 2,000 books to be transported to various stops such as grade schools and parks. During the two summers it operated, the truck visited Grant, Garfield, Jefferson, Lincoln, Roosevelt, McKinley, and Westwood schools; Allendale; Evansville; Dempsey Acres; Mills; the airport; and a point five miles north of Casper on the old Salt Creek Highway. In the summer of 1956, during the ten weeks that Howard drove the truck, she circulated 6,000 books.

New Construction

By far, Margaret Burke's greatest achievement during her tenure as Head Librarian was facilitating the construction of a new wing on the old Carnegie building and its 1925 addition. An undated news clipping credits Burke with being "primarily responsible for getting the [Wyoming] state legislature to pass a law permitting bond issues to be floated to build new libraries." This she did in the late 1940s, and the Natrona County Public Library was the first of Wyoming's libraries to take advantage of the legislation.

In October 1945, the library's Trustees had a lengthy discussion about a new wing for the library. By mid-1946 they began to consult with Casper architect Leon C. Goodrich about the design. Nothing came of this until the summer of 1948, when Board members met with County Commissioners to discuss a $200,000 bond for additional space at the library. However, this was tabled in October 1948 because the Board wanted to be included as an equal partner in a proposed improvement plan created by the Casper Long-Range Planning Board. In pursuing this possibility, Library Board President Charles Rose and Board Secretary Billy Johnson sent a letter on October 13, 1948, to the County Commissioners. The letter stated that the library did not wish to ask for a bond issue at that time because, in Johnson's words, "It is the desire of the Library Board...to work in all aspects in harmony with the planning group." He went on to reiterate that the "Board is convinced of the necessity for the expansion of the facilities of the library." Long-Range Planning Board Chairman Harold H. Healy responded graciously on October 21, 1948, "I was instructed to write expressing in part at least our appreciation to you as public minded citizens as well as faithful public officials who are interested, in common with the members of the Planning Board, in both the near term and long range welfare of the community."

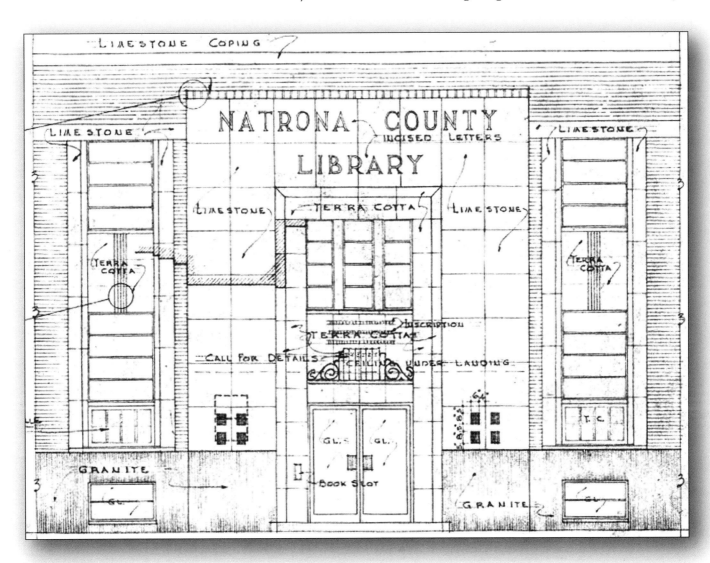

The north façade and entrance of the 1952 addition shown in this architect's drawing, though modified, are still visible today.
Drawing from NCPL files.

No further action occurred until March 1950, when the Library Board announced that it would seek a $260,000 bond that August to construct a new addition to the library's inadequate facilities. By this time, the original Carnegie building was forty years old and the 1925 wing was twenty-five. Leon C. Goodrich would again be the project's architect. On March 25, 1950, Board President James G. Crawford wrote a letter to the County Commissioners requesting that Natrona County residents approve the $260,000 bond issue in August 1950 in order to add a fireproof wing to the current library structures. The bond election was held and passed that August, but the Trustees waited a year before approving Goodrich's blueprints for the new wing that included a 7,500-square-foot main level, the same size basement, and a 3,900-square-foot mezzanine. This wing, however, would not resemble the existing building. The brick exterior would be cream- and buff-colored with terra cotta trim while the interior would have a terrazzo staircase, red oak columns, doors, and paneling, and cork tile for the floor on the main level.

On June 4, 1952, only two contractors, Riedesel-Lowe and Rognstad & Olsen, met at Goodrich's office to bid on the proposed new wing. The successful firm was Rognstad & Olsen, whose bid of $289,000 was the lower of the two. Rognstad & Olsen began excavating for the new building in August 1952. When the project was completed in late 1953, it included $20,000 in new furniture and a remodeling of the old portions of the library, including a petroleum room that represented Burke's dream and long-standing ambition. Again showing her ability to enlist the cooperation of other agencies in the area, Burke persuaded the Wyoming Geological Association to donate $2,100 to assist in the creation of the petroleum room. By 1961, this room contained 1,400 books, memoirs, surveys, maps and charts, reports, monographs, pamphlets, interim reports, indexes, circulars, and bulletins, many of which were produced by the United States Geological Survey. The 1963 annual report claimed the

GEOLOGISTS SUPPORT LIBRARY: The library committee of the Wyoming Geological Association meeting in the Natrona County Public Library with Head Librarian LaFrances Sullivan. From left are John Albanese, chairman, R. L. Nelson and W. W. Stewart. The WGA cooperates with the library regarding the earth science collection.

Undated news clipping in NCPL scrapbook.
Reprinted with permission from the Casper
Star-Tribune.

Main floor and mezzanine of the 1952 addition, looking east. The entrance was left of the mezzanine stairs.
Photo from NCPL files.

"Petroleum Section has been well used and we feel the library does a valuable service to the oil industry of Casper and vicinity." In 1964, the Wyoming Geological Association started paying for Wyoming-related well-log data to go into the library's petroleum collection. In 1967, the library boasted that its petroleum collection was one of the "best in the state."

The new wing also made possible a larger children's department. Decorated in shell-pink and blue, the new room had shelving that Rognstad & Olsen provided at a cost of $590.

The old children's room was then used mostly for storage, showing movies, and conducting summer story hour. Story hour was always a popular attraction for preschool children; during the early 1950s, Children's Librarian Edna Lockhart added an annual puppet show.

On January 4, 1954, Burke and her staff held an open house from 1:00 p.m. to 6:00 p.m. to display the new library facilities. An untitled manuscript from January 5, 1954, noted, "Perhaps the first thing that patrons and other visitors remark about when entering the library is

North face of the 1952 addition with the original Carnegie building still standing on the west end. Photo circa 1960 from NCPL files.

the feeling of repose, peace and quiet." Burke wrote in a short article published in *Library Journal* in 1955, "The library gives the reader a feeling that here is a place where he likes to come and stay, where he is comfortable and uncrowded, and where the atmosphere is friendly." She also commented to the *Casper Tribune-Herald* that the new addition had made it much more pleasant for library staff to conduct their daily work.

The one disquieting aspect of the new wing was the manner in which patrons used the new mezzanine. Noisy crowds of young people chose to congregate there after school and later in the evenings. In April 1957, Burke told the Trustees that she was considering hiring a college student at one dollar per hour to patrol the mezzanine. While she did not pursue this course of action, the problem would haunt her replacement, LaFrances Sullivan, in the years to come.

Margaret Burke lived only a few months after talking to the Trustees about the mezzanine situation. In mid-October 1957, after working at the county library for nearly twenty years, she died suddenly at the age of sixty-five. Among the things that Burke did for the library during her time as Head Librarian was to hire LaFrances Sullivan as the library's cataloger.

On the Cusp of Change

Sullivan started working at the library in June 1950 for $180 per month. After Burke died, the Library Trustees quickly offered Sullivan the job as Head Librarian at $500 per month. She had excellent credentials. A native of North Dakota, she graduated from Colorado State Teacher's College, and then received a master's degree from the University of California. She also received library training at the University of Southern California and became the librarian at Irving Junior High School in the historic

MRS. HAROLD L. SULLIVAN

LaFrances Sullivan instituted technological changes at the library.
Photo published October 27, 1957, in the Casper Tribune Herald and Star, *reprinted with permission* **from the Casper Star-Tribune.**

Sugar House section of Salt Lake City. After Irving Junior High, she served as the librarian at West High School in Salt Lake City. Once at the Natrona County Public Library, she "carried on with untiring energy," in Billy Johnson's words.

Sullivan was Head Librarian during a time when the library balanced on the cusp of major changes, of which she was clearly aware. In a late 1965 conversation with a correspondent from the *Casper Star-Tribune*, she remarked, "The county library is now in the transition stage from a place where a person could sit in silence and read and think, to a center for research and a multitude of public services."

Microfilm and Music

Sullivan changed the way the library was used with the introduction of two relatively untried technologies. The first of these was microfilm. In her 1960 annual report, she announced that the newspaper-storage space in the basement of the old portion of the library was completely full. Consequently, she purchased a microfilm machine and a storage case. She also planned to purchase the current year's editions of local newspapers on microfilm and then start adding two to three years of back issues each year. In her 1961 report, she noted, "Of all the firsts for 1961

the microfilm reader might be said to be the most important thing to happen to the library since the new building was completed." By the end of 1962, she announced that the library had nineteen rolls of microfilm covering newspapers from 1889 to 1916. In 1966, both students and adults were using the microfilm for school assignments and genealogical research. A year later, the library began to order magazines on microfilm.

Sullivan's second venture into non-book formats was with recorded music. In 1963, she purchased a stereo record player with money from an anonymous donor. A medical doctor had given the money to honor Grace Bean, a former music teacher of his who taught in Shoshoni starting in 1907 and in Casper starting in 1931. Sullivan noted that while she was now purchasing records with the library's

QUICK COPY: Mrs. Norman Stover, an employe of the Natrona County Public Library, makes a copy of part of the front page of the Saturday, Jan. 6, 1923, Casper Daily Tribune. Library patrons may have copies of microfilmed materials made for 15 cents apiece.

Beverly (Diehl) Stover, pictured above, later became the head of the library's technical services department. Published January 7, 1968, reprinted with permission from the Casper Star-Tribune.

BORROWS RECORD: Mrs. Claude Murray, left, is the first person to borrow a record from the Natrona County Public Library. Mrs. Stanley Winter, a librarian, checks out the disc. A charge of 10 cents is made on each record to help defray wear and tear.

Undated news clipping in NCPL scrapbook. Reprinted with permission from the Casper Star-Tribune.

acquisitions money, the Casper Association of Childhood Education had also donated $25 to buy children's records. In her 1964 annual report to the Trustees, Sullivan wrote, "The new stereo phonograph has been welcomed by the public. Many patrons have used it while spending time in the library." She continued, "One man often visited during his lunch hour, a student listened to poetry in conjunction with an assignment, and another listened while taking a study break. Children have been delighted with the juvenile records."

Youth Services and Challenges

Several of Sullivan's activities were continuations of Burke's earlier endeavors. One of these was the ongoing Bookworm program that Burke had coordinated with Flo Rogers from the county school district. In 1964, the school district decided to drop the program, so Sullivan offered

to accept it as a part of the library's responsibility. At the May 29, 1964, Board meeting, the Library Trustees noted a letter of gratitude to the library from Maurice F. Griffith, Superintendent of the County School District. In the following months, Sullivan hired Sue Frech to be the new "Bookworm Lady." The program was popular and provided an excellent opportunity for young people to use and enjoy their public library. In the summer of 1965, the library provided a selection of thirty-six books for the young readers enrolled in the Bookworm program. Among these were *Princess and the Lion, Little Plum, A Golden Touch, The Woodrow Wilson Story: An Idealist in Politics,* and *Hibernian Nights.*

In 1966, Frech hosted six visits to the library for a total of 1,500 Bookworm children. In the 1968-1969 school year, large numbers of students from area schools were bused to the library to participate in the program.

Other children's programs were popular and successful while Sullivan was the Head Librarian. Story hour continued under the direction of Marie Compton and Dorothy Mills with the assistance of two high school girls. Story hour took place every Wednesday at 2:00 p.m. with the children

Sue Frech became "The Bookworm Lady" when the library took over the Bookworm program from the school district in 1964.
Photo from NCPL files.

divided into a four- and five-year-old group and a six-year-old group. The average weekly attendance was between fifty and sixty youngsters. In her 1963 annual report, Sullivan described the children's portion of the library, the junior department, as being "an interesting and pleasant place to visit" with its brightly decorated bulletin boards and occasional artwork from local elementary schools. She also noted that every May the children's department hosted a library orientation for all of the school district's first-graders.

The type of student visit that did not please Sullivan, however, was the afternoon and evening gatherings of young people who would rush into the library during the winter months and head to the mezzanine "for every excuse available but for study." These visits tested Sullivan's patience. In 1960, she said, "While we welcome the young people and are eager to help them, they present a problem of discipline and vandalism. The damage done to the library proper and the book collection has been severe." In her 1961 report, she labeled the situation as a teenage problem that seemed to be "a continual one." During that year, Sullivan tied the misconduct to a second issue: overcrowding caused when too many students visited the library after school to complete homework assignments. They would "flock to the [library] and occupy all the tables and chairs."

At a Board meeting in November 1962, Sullivan elaborated on this dual nature of the student situation. According to the Board's minutes, Sullivan contended, "The lack of seating capacity and supervision" exacerbated the negative behaviors of the high school students who used the library in the evenings. While it would be several years before a solution was found to the challenge of overcrowding (another library construction project), Sullivan suggested an immediate remedy – the hiring of a night supervisor. Within a month after talking to the Board members, she employed a man on a

thirty-day trial basis. However, he quit after one night because, as Sullivan lamented, the situation was more than he could endure.

A Changing Collection

Another challenge Sullivan faced was a significant loss of library materials. In December 1961, according to a newspaper clipping, the library conducted an inventory of its book collections, the result being that "a staggering amount of books were found to be missing." The number missing was 1,600, which at the time represented approximately 3 percent of the library's overall book holdings. In October 1964, Sullivan told a *Casper Star-Tribune* staff writer that the library was missing $3,000 worth of books, all stolen, while other volumes had "pages torn out, pages scribbled over with obscenities, pages cleverly cut out with razor blades, damaged magazines, books with graphs, tables and illustrations rent from them." She also explained that automobile repair and firearms books were the ones most commonly damaged.

Despite the theft and vandalism of books, Sullivan sounded a positive note when she observed that library users had shifted their reading habits to more serious books. A February 1961 newspaper article announced, "During the past few years library patrons have been checking out fewer westerns and who-done-its and concentrating more on science and biographical works. Students are especially interested in science." To Sullivan, the shift meant that her staff needed to consult book lists more carefully and then to purchase materials on a large variety of subjects. By the end of the 1960s, the *Casper Star-Tribune* reported that the most popular books in the library were those on a variety of how-to subjects such as carpentry, cooking, farming, automobiles, and medicine. This reflected the statement Sullivan made in 1965, when she claimed that the Natrona County Public Library had become "a center for research."

Overcrowding and Facility Changes

In 1960, Sullivan reported that the Wyoming books, numbering 850 volumes, were housed in an old portion of the library with inadequate shelving. In mid-1968, Sullivan had the collection moved to the mezzanine and then held an open house on November 24 to show off the Wyoming collection's new quarters. An invitation to members of the Natrona County Historical Society and the Pioneer Association stated, "This collection in the past was housed in a tiny room in the old wing. It has recently been moved to a special room in the newer wing." Edness Kimball Wilkins, Wyoming state legislator, Natrona County historian, and daughter of former Casper Mayor Wilson S. Kimball, was among those who attended the open house.

Moving the Wyoming collection to the mezzanine was only a small and belated indication of the congestion that the county library was facing. The lack of space had become a painful issue for all who worked in or visited the library throughout the 1960s. A 1961 *Casper Tribune-Herald* article reported, "The old section of the [library] is badly in need of repairs and before long more room for both books and readers will be needed." Later in the year the same newspaper exclaimed, "The old public library with the ostrich egg dome has got to go." But to some, this was not an acceptable solution. In her 1962 annual report, Sullivan asserted, "The original building with its white dome and beautiful vines...is a landmark." Landmark or not, less than ten years after the library's 1952 wing was completed, discussion of how to alleviate the public library's congestion had begun again.

In the same 1961 *Tribune-Herald* article stating that the old library building "has got to go," the correspondent wrote that Library Trustees Stella Russell, Billy Johnson, and Charles L. Rose had started conversing with the County Commissioners about the matter. The article also reported that the bond for the 1954 wing had just been paid off. A movement toward a new facility had been initiated.

At the end of 1961, the Board of Trustees began to discuss obtaining an easement to the parcel of land immediately to the south of the library, where an old American Legion building existed at the time. This land was owned by Oscar Whitlock. Whitlock also owned the Tip Top building to the east of the library. In early 1962, the Board hired Libraries Unlimited for $500 to assist in planning a new building. At the

Members of the Casper Historical Society and the Pioneer Association visited in the library before viewing the library's special Wyoming collection, which had been moved to more spacious quarters in the library's newer wing. Pictured at left is Wyoming State Legislator Edness Kimball Wilkins, a member of the Historical Society. Sue Frech is pouring punch. Photo from NCPL files.

same time, the County Commissioners met with Whitlock to discuss an easement on his property. Before the end of 1963, the Trustees met with Whitlock and his attorney, E. L. McCary. By this time, library officials had decided that they would have the Carnegie building and its 1925 wing razed to make room for a new addition.

In the library's 1964 annual report, Sullivan wrote that she and the Board members had approached the County Commissioners about the possibility of having a bond issue put before voters. The Commissioners had been reluctant to set a time for the bond election. The Trustees expressed some doubt about particulars regarding a bond issue. When discussing the idea of including the cost of a bookmobile in the bond's sum, Board minutes on December 8, 1965, recorded that "bookmobile service perilous to a building program might affect a negative vote for a bond issue." By 1967, the Board had reversed itself on this issue and had decided that a bookmobile "would be the most satisfactory method of service to outlying areas…offering a vital up-to-date and convenient means of securing materials to read."

The idea of expanding and improving the library's facilities moved forward. In February 1966, the Library Trustees hired Goodrich and Wilking to design a floor plan and architectural sketches for a new building. The new facility would be 21,400 square feet and would feature both large and small meeting rooms. The addition of meeting rooms echoed Billy Johnson's contention that one of the reasons for building the 1925 wing was to meet a "considerable demand [for] a room suitable for all kinds of meetings." The total cost of $542,000 included razing the original Carnegie structure and the 1925 addition, constructing the new wing, and purchasing a new bookmobile. The Trustees would request $410,000 in bond funds and $132,000 in federal money under a program called the Library Services Act.

Dorothy Mill, Elva Shoultz, and other staff members strove to deal with flooding in the deteriorating Carnegie building.
Photo from NCPL files.

The Library Trustees and County Commissioners agreed on a bond election date of March 7, 1967. A spirited debate exploded regarding the need for a new library building. Two reasons for a new addition were the extensive damage and deterioration in the older sections of the basement and the seemingly endless roof problems. A library fact sheet released in 1967 stated, "Flooding in the basement from broken water lines and water back up from the street into the basement makes one section of it unusable for storage. In other parts… the painting has peeled off and the walls are damaged by water and mildew." The roof situation was equally depressing: "The skylights, the overhang and the roof leak. During heavy rains and snows pans and buckets are set up around on the main floor to catch the water." In several articles, the *Casper Star-Tribune* took

GIVE THE BOY A SUIT THAT FITS

This cartoon from the March 5, 1967, Casper Star-Tribune urged voters to approve a bond issue to improve the library facility.
Illustration by Ray Grahn, reprinted with permission from the Casper Star-Tribune.

more tables and quiet rooms for independent research." He concluded, "For these reasons I urge support of the proposed bond issue."

In opposition, one county resident spoke out in an editorial, "Lack of space has been mentioned by reporters. However, in parts of the new building there is ample room to drive two or three large elephants about." A letter to phone-bank volunteers who were to make calls on behalf of the bond's passage acknowledged the existence of opposition, warning, "If you should call a particularly recalcitrant voter, try to terminate the conversation as gracefully as possible without irritating him to begin an anti-library campaign on his own."

At the end of 1966, a group of library advocates organized a Friends association to support the bond issue. On May 22, 1994, an article by Charlotte Babcock in the *Casper Star-Tribune* reported that this group, "whose chairman was John Albanese, decided that it was apparent that the library needed 'friends' more that [*sic*] ever, and the 'Friends of the Library' became official."

On March 5, 1967, the *Casper Star-Tribune* defined reasons to approve the issue, "From many standpoints – the need for space, the deterioration of the old wing, and the cause of architectural unity and efficiency of operation – there is reason to say yes to the bond issue." Despite what the *Casper Star-Tribune* called a "strong campaign conducted by proponents," the bond issue failed. A light turnout of only 3,900 voters went to the polls, and of those who voted, 2,100 voted against the issue while only 1,800 were in favor.

It was time for library officials to return to the drawing board to review their plans. At the April 1967 meeting, Board members recorded that they would continue efforts to secure the necessary funds to build a new library addition. By the end of the year, they had determined to request that, if land for the library expansion

the library's side in the controversy. One article contended, "Repairing Old Library Called Hopeless Cause," while another declared, "Library Pressed for Space."

In an editorial in favor of passing the bond, Dean Morgan Junior High School art teacher Norma Bathurst wrote, "During the past year while doing research for a paper, I spent most evenings of several months in the Natrona County Public Library. I soon found out that if I wished to find a place to work, I should be there not later than 6 o'clock in the evening." Doug Jones, a high school debater, added, "I have seen the leaky roof, the torn tiles, and the poorly lighted recesses in which much of the resource material is kept. There also exists a need for

Fred Johnson, President of the Friends of the Library, presided over a 1967 ceremony honoring Verna Keyes, designer of the Wyoming state flag. The original is currently displayed on the second floor of the library.
Photo from NCPL files.

could be acquired, the County Commissioners approve a bond election to purchase additional land and to pay for a new library structure. In August 1969, the Trustees would again present a bond issue to voters.

Community Involvement

The library's involvement in community events prior to the election underscored its value to the community. On December 9, 1967, the Friends of the Library sponsored a ceremony to honor Verna Keyes, a Casper woman who designed the Wyoming state flag in 1916. The event featured special guests Wyoming Secretary of State Thyra Thomson, Wyoming State Representative William Swanton, Wyoming United States Congressman William Henry Harrison, and James Fagan, who stood in for Wyoming United States Senator Gale McGee. The master of ceremonies for the event was Fred Johnson, President of the Friends organization. The program included an invocation, the posting of the United States flag by members of the Casper Troopers Drum and Bugle Corps, the Pledge of Allegiance, speeches by dignitaries, and presentation of a plaque to Keyes. The American Legion, Boy Scouts of America, Girl Scouts of America, Campfire Girls, Daughters of the American Revolution, and Natrona County Historical Society all participated in the ceremony.

Another opportunity to promote the library was its participation in the Casper Downtown Merchants' annual Crazy Days celebration in 1968 – a time when merchants throughout the downtown area displayed samples of their merchandise on storefront sidewalks. Sue Frech, Adult Services Director, put together a plan designed to increase the library's presence at Crazy Days and the Casper Day parade that initiated the Central Wyoming Fair and Rodeo. In a 1968 fact sheet titled "Adult Services at Natrona County Public Library," Frech wrote, "The Downtown Merchants were pleased to have the library share this activity. Books were checked out from table and [book carts] on the sidewalk in front of the library. A gaily decorated puppet booth was used for young people to attract attention with tambourines, bells and triangles…. A bright high-scooter bike ridden up and down the sidewalk attracted many patrons. Our young librarians wore crazy costumes of the 1930s vintage. Radio stations KATI, KVOC and KTWO covered the activity and KTWO-TV reviewed it on several news casts."

For the 1969 Crazy Days and fair and rodeo events, library staff decorated a dune buggy as an outer-space "blastmobile" for the fair and rodeo parade. The vehicle displayed a sign that read, "Drop in…Check out…Turn on," and featured moon maidens and spacemen checking out books. As a final touch, the library borrowed the Laramie County Public Library's bookmobile and decorated it to advertise the Natrona County Library at the fair and rodeo celebration.

A Successful Bond Issue

Laying the groundwork for the new election required more than a year, but at the May 1969 Board meeting, the Library Board members announced that they were ready to pursue a

$1.1 million bond issue. Goals of this issue would be to buy land, replace the Carnegie building, and purchase a bookmobile.

August 26, 1969, was set as the election date. The firm of Gariety and Payne was in charge of publicizing the bond issue. As publicity coordinator, Frech created flyers and brochures and organized precinct chair people to share the message regarding the need for a new library. She also used the Laramie County Library's bookmobile to raise awareness in various locations around the city and county. She arranged for prominent community residents to do radio and television endorsements. She took slide presentations to various service clubs and visited other boards in the county with members of the Library Board.

The *Casper Star-Tribune* ran a series of library photographs with captions that highlighted the facility's inadequate conditions. One photo showed the microfilm machine hidden away in an obscure location. Another showed useless space in the basement. One caption stated that the library needed soft chairs to replace the old hardwood ones that existed at that time.

Library employees, including Carol Puettman, Janet Dinsmore, and Carl Van, joined downtown merchants in their Crazy Days promotions.
Photo from NCPL files.

On August 24, 1969, the *Star-Tribune* ran an article with the headline, "Voters Can See Conditions During Open House."

According to a fact sheet on the bond issue, conditions were deplorable: "The wiring and plumbing...are in bad condition." The roof was in danger of collapsing under the pressure of heavy rain or snow, and the basement flooded often. "The old wing has reached the state in its life when it is physically unfit to be used." Even if the deteriorated plumbing and wiring were repaired, "We will still have an old building." Underscoring the change from what had once been Casper's beautiful Carnegie library with its 1925 addition, the fact sheet continued,

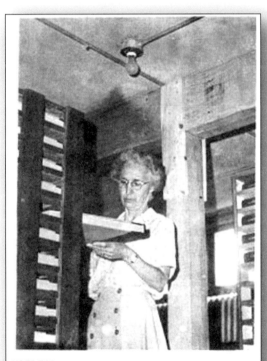

USELESS SPACE: The basement of the old wing of the Natrona County Public Library can be used only for storage. A year ago the building was shored up with beams as seen here. Librarian Mildred Morse gets out a bound copy of the Casper Tribune. Newspapers and bound periodicals are kept in the basement where the public can't get them and they are inconveniently located for librarians. A new library wing, which will be obtained by passage of the $1,100,000 bond issue Tuesday, will provide safe and convenient storage for these volumes.

Published August 21, 1969, in the
Casper Star-Tribune.
Reprinted with permission.

"Junior department users must traipse through the poorly lighted, sometimes damp old junior room to the far west confines to use the lavatory facilities which themselves are old, unsightly, and designed for adults instead of small children."

To correct these conditions, the library proposed to purchase 50,000 square feet of land from Oscar Whitlock at a price of $275,000, raze the old library wings and the American Legion building, build a 23,000-square-foot structure where the old library had been, purchase a bookmobile that could hold up to 4,000 books, and use the leftover space for parking and beautification.

Voters approved the $1.1 million bond issue on August 26, 1969, with 2,300 votes for and 1,600 against. John Burke, one of the County Commissioners, commented with considerable foresight the day after the election, "I feel this is the last chance we have to expand the present facilities in their present place."

Two days before the election, LaFrances Sullivan died. Shortly before her death, Trustee James Crawford said, "Her stature is that of a giant, like a beacon lighting the mind's way. Modest in her personal life, clear-eyed, and sure in professional life." She was ideally suited for her job at the public library. Several times she requested that the Board not grant her a salary increase so that they might have a little more money for the other library employees. In addition, she always seemed to be available near the circulation or children's desks to speak with patrons, and she was very encouraging of others who were considering becoming librarians. This author spoke with her at the library in October 1968, and among her last words to him was praise for the public-service opportunities inherent in the library profession. Sullivan's funeral took place the day of the library's bond election, and to honor her, the Board of Trustees closed the library for the day.

Summary

At the time of Sullivan's death, the library stood at a juncture in its history. The staff had grown from twelve in 1950 (the year Margaret Burke hired Sullivan to be an assistant librarian) to twenty-one in 1968. Among the library employees in 1969 were a head librarian, a reference librarian, a cataloger, a periodicals librarian, a children's librarian, an assistant children's employee, a bookkeeper, two full-time circulation-desk workers, a branch librarian, two shelvers, and a janitor. The library's growth and use were restricted by cramped facilities, deterioration in the older sections of the library with persistent roof problems and leaky basement walls, and lack of parking other than at meters on Durbin and Second streets. Yet the library was open Monday through Saturday, sixty-nine hours for adults and fifty-six hours for children. It also remained receptive to change in technology and community needs.

LaFrances Sullivan, Margaret Burke, and the head librarians before them had assisted in laying substantial groundwork for an increasingly active public library in central Wyoming. The replacement of the old Carnegie library would be the launching point for the Natrona County Public Library's leap into the modern world. Sullivan stated in November 1965 that the Natrona County Public Library was moving into a period of transition. She had an accurate sense that important changes had begun, although she did not live to see the results.

Chapter Five: The Introduction of Computer Technology
1970-1993

*A good public library is the lifeblood of any community: It ensures that
all people, from all walks of life, have access to the information and ideas
they need to learn and grow, to solve problems, and to dream.*

James A. Michener

Natrona County was changing. Its population was growing, particularly in the Casper area. The oil industry was beginning to revive and soon would boom because of the restrictive action of the Organization of Petroleum Exporting Countries (OPEC), which led to increases in the price of oil and heightened emphasis on finding more petroleum-producing areas in the United States.

Higher oil prices also stimulated producers to squeeze more petroleum out of older domestic fields such as Salt Creek in northern Natrona County. Coal and uranium exploration grew also. The pace of economic growth in Natrona County quickened in the 1970s, which meant more tax revenue for the county. Population growth increased demand for public services such as

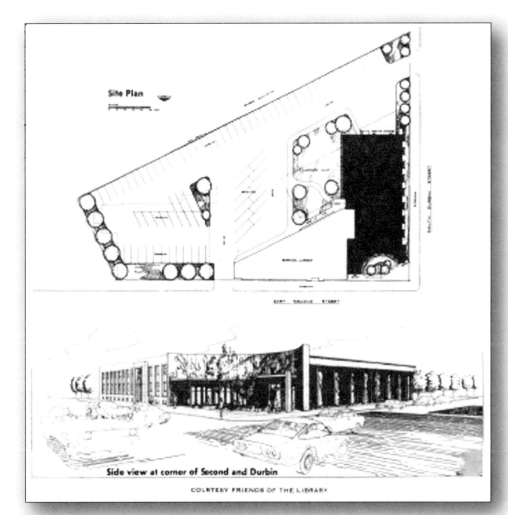

An early site plan shows how the new structure (black area on the right) would replace the original Carnegie building and the 1925 addition.
Diagram from 1969 election brochure published by the Friends of the Library.

Side view at corner of Second and Durbin

COURTESY FRIENDS OF THE LIBRARY

Kenneth Dowlin became Director in 1969 and oversaw library construction projects in both Casper and Edgerton.
Photo from NCPL files.

schools, public safety, transportation, recreational opportunities, and public facilities. Increased wages and the establishment by many energy companies of district headquarters in Casper created a more metropolitan community, fueling a desire for the cultural amenities of more urban areas.

For the public library, change began in the early 1970s with the arrival of a new library director and a new building to replace the old Carnegie structure and the 1925 wing. After enduring hard economic times and numerous

---

Spotlight: 1970
Natrona County Population: 51,300
Casper Population: 49,800

Natrona County Public Library Facts
Library Director: Kenneth Dowlin
Library Collection: 77,400
Circulation: 211,300
Budget: $151,000
Board Members: John P. Albanese,
    Frank L. Bowron, James G. Craw-
    ford, Nona Muller, Lois Shickich

---

budget cuts, the library would now be able to enhance community outreach, provide broader services, and most of all, institute technological advances. An overarching theme connecting the last years of LaFrances Sullivan's work to the endeavors of future library directors is the successful integration of new technologies with traditional library services.

A New Library Building

In June 1969, anticipating passage of the August bond issue, the Library Trustees hired Henry Therkildsen as the architect for a new library construction project. Head Librarian LaFrances Sullivan died two days before the election after being extremely ill for two months. The Library Trustees appointed librarian Mildred Morse as the library's Acting Librarian until a new director could be hired. After the bond issue passed, the Trustees selected Kenneth Dowlin of Arvada, Colorado, to be the Director. Dowlin came to his new position in December 1969 with a set of priorities in mind, among which was the development of an efficient physical plant. However, the construction of the new library facilities proved challenging to the new Director and the Board of Trustees.

In the spring of 1970, the Trustees hired Astro Wrecking to raze the old Carnegie building, the 1925 addition, and the adjacent Casper American Legion building that the library had purchased with 1969 bond funds. Astro Wrecking began its demolition work in May 1970 and finished in late June.

On February 17, 1971, Library Trustees John Albanese, Frank Bowron, James Crawford, and Nona Muller met in a special session to open bids for the construction of a new two-story wing with basement on the site of the old library structures. Four construction companies presented bids, the lowest being Louis C. Rognstad's for slightly under $700,000. The Trustees accepted Rognstad as their contractor.

Following demolition of the Carnegie structure and the building to the south of the library (top photo), the new addition included a distinctive curved entrance (bottom photo).
Photos from NCPL files.

As with the building of the original Carnegie library, construction did not proceed smoothly. First, a major difficulty arose with the bricks that Therkildsen planned for the building's exterior. In May 1971, the architect told the Board members that he had specified an Apache-colored brick. In August, however, the Trustees learned that the wrong color brick had been shipped. This caused Rognstad to delay work until late 1971. Then, in June 1972, a second major dilemma arose when the Trustees discovered that the quality of the new building's carpet was unacceptable. It took the carpet supplier, Burke Furniture in Casper, nearly six months to remedy the situation.

Despite a series of lesser problems that occurred during the construction work, Rognstad had made enough progress by mid-September 1972 that Library Trustees, staff, and the Friends held a festival to celebrate the new building. The celebration started on September 14 and continued through September 24, featuring exhibits, entertainment, demonstrations, and a special children's day. A formal dedication ceremony concluded the series of events.

Kenneth Dowlin also oversaw the construction of a new branch library for the residents of the neighboring communities of Midwest and Edgerton. The 1969 bond provided the funds to build the facility at Edgerton. Architect Therkildsen estimated that the branch's new structure would cost $23,000 to construct, but at a meeting with prospective contractors in October 1970, all bids proved to be much higher than Therkildsen's estimate. The Board then requested a second round of meetings with construction firms. In November 1970, Herb Blake of Edgerton's Blake Construction presented an offer to build the branch library for just under $24,000, a bid that the Trustees accepted. The Edgerton Branch Library opened at the end of 1971. In 1978, it became known as the Mark J. Davis Memorial Branch, in honor of the late Board member Mark Davis.

The Mark J. Davis Branch library serves the communities of Midwest and Edgerton, located approximately 40 miles from the county seat.
Photo from NCPL files.

The "Reading Roustabout" Bookmobile

Kenneth Dowlin also had the honor of presiding over the purchase of the library's first bookmobile with earmarked funds from the 1969 library bond. The library purchased a $24,000 converted school bus that was christened the "Reading Roustabout" in January 1971. This vehicle traveled throughout Natrona County, making as many as thirty stops per week.

A colorful experience of one of its earliest drivers, Marilyn Lewis, illustrates the level of service as the Reading Roustabout traveled to Natrona County's outlying populations. Arriving one day at her normal stop of Alcova, Lewis cheerfully accepted a shipment of snakes, which she took home to keep for several days. Then, taking this special cargo to Arminto aboard the bookmobile, she exchanged the snakes for a box of mice. Library records do not state what she did with the mice, but it is clear that she had established an excellent rapport with her patrons. Such reports show the public-service nature of the bookmobile's outreach operations.

New Technology: Computers, Cable, and County Records

Dowlin was most noted for his forward-looking view of supporting library services with technology, including microfilm, computers, and cable television. As he stated in a 1974 report on the library's use of such technologies, Dowlin had long thought of connecting libraries to television because he felt, "It is important that libraries become familiar with [television's] uses and misuses. Cable television is not only a fast growing industry; it is one which may have long range ramifications for us in the library business." In February 1972, after contracting with the Wyoming Cable Television Company for the use of Channel 12, the library went on the air with borrowed equipment. He remarked in a follow-up report that "the experiment was exciting."

The Reading Roustabout allowed library services to reach all corners of the county.
Photo from NCPL files.

In March 1971, the Library Trustees approved Dowlin's request to buy equipment so that by 1974, the Director had established a television studio in the library's basement.

The space that became this studio has an interesting history. When the 1972 addition was being constructed, the contractors had planned to dig a large hole in which to construct the supporting subsurface walls and columns for the new library's first and second floors. Once the supporting work was done, the contractors were going to backfill the space below the first floor. When the Library Trustees heard about the hole that was to be backfilled, they saw an opportunity to expand the new building's basement. Trula Cooper then visited the County Commissioners' offices and convinced the Commissioners to approve the creation of the extra basement space. Being a very determined member of the Library Board, Cooper paved the way for the basement expansion, which gave Dowlin the opportunity to have the space necessary for his television studio.

To honor the Board's longest-serving member, Billy Johnson, the Library Trustees named the new facility the Billy Johnson Memorial Studio. Library employees used the studio for programs such as a children's series called "Growing Up with Stories," book review sessions known as "Between the Covers," and holiday specials for young people. Public service groups also took advantage of the studio; for example, the Casper League of Women Voters broadcast a political candidates forum in 1974.

On December 13, 1971, the *Casper Star-Tribune* quoted Dowlin as boasting that the

Natrona County Public Library had just become the first library in the United States to combine cable television with public library service. Until Dowlin's experiment, library use of cable television had never been "more than hinted at."

Dowlin also used television to facilitate an outreach program called Video Reference Service. He contracted with Casper's cable system to use a television channel to answer telephone reference questions. The reference department installed a television camera mounted on a stand above a small table. When a patron called with a question, a member of the reference staff found

Director Kenneth Dowlin, shown here in the Billy Johnson Memorial Studio, believed that television could complement the library rather than compete with it.
Photo from NCPL files.

a book to answer the patron's query, and then opened that book to the relevant page and placed the book on the table below the camera. The patron then tuned into the library's cable channel and viewed the answer to his or her question. The Video Reference Service began in January 1972, and that year's annual report to the Wyoming State Library stated that the Natrona County Public Library had "pioneered the first library service via a cable television system in the nation."

The creation of an operation called the County Records System is perhaps Dowlin's most enduring technological innovation. This program entailed microfilming all county government records and providing computer-based indexing to the microfilm. In January 1973, Dowlin asked the Library Trustees for a budget to design and develop this system. Several months later, he presented to the County Commissioners a twenty-minute video explaining how the system operated. By October, the library had hired two technicians and two clerks to implement the system. By early April 1974, County Records System staff members had microfilmed all the Sheriff's Department records and were inputting this data into a computer, while simultaneously starting to microfilm the Clerk of Court's records.

Art for the Library

Dowlin tendered his resignation in January 1975 and left on March 1 to become the Director for the Pikes Peak Regional Library District in Colorado Springs, Colorado. Shortly before his departure, an impressive sculpture titled "Prometheus" was placed at the library's northwest entrance. The bronze statue was created by sculptor and University of Wyoming professor Robert Russin in his studio in Florence, Italy.

This public art project began in November 1971, when the Library Trustees stated that they wished to have a well-known artist produce a sculpture to adorn the library's main entrance. Two prominent local citizens, Tom Stroock and Jack

This ad appearing in a "TV Facts" insert in the newspaper described Video Reference Service for library patrons. Clipping from NCPL files used with permission of Bresnan Communications.

Prometheus has adorned the library's north entrance since 1975. This photo shows the statue as originally cast, before vandalism provided the sculptor an opportunity to redesign the flames.
Photo from NCPL files.

Rosenthal, joined with Russin to find the funds necessary to support such a project. Within a three-year period, seventeen individuals and nineteen corporate donors had given money to finance Prometheus.

Once Russin finished his work and the large sculpture arrived at the library, the Friends of the Library hosted a dedication ceremony on February 8, 1975. The ceremony featured Library Board member Art Volk unveiling the statue, followed by a reception in the library's new Crawford Room, named for former longtime Board member James G. Crawford. In 2007, Volk and fellow Board members Trula Cooper and Frank "Pinky" Ellis recalled that the acquisition and dedication of Prometheus was a highlight of their time on the Board.

New Leadership and Added Computer Functions

For a brief period after Dowlin left the Natrona County Public Library, librarian Elizabeth Fuller served as the Acting Director. Then, in the summer of 1975, John Peters of Bloomington, Indiana, became the library's new Director, the eighth since the opening of the library in 1910. During Peters' tenure, the library began to scale back its public television operations; the first to go was the Video Reference Service. In a summary report dated November 11, 1976, Christopher Jones, head of the library's technological operations, stated that use of this unique reference service had dropped significantly. In an undated memo to the Library Trustees, he admitted that the reference service needed "some revitalization." The program languished and disappeared without further attention.

John Peters concentrated his efforts on staffing issues, including the introduction of computerized circulation functions.
Photo from NCPL files.

Long-time staff member Lida (Krans) Volin shows off the library's first circulation desk computer.
Photo from NCPL files.

In addition to the cancellation of the Video Reference Service, the programs offered through the Johnson Memorial Studio began to falter. In his November 11, 1976, report, Jones hinted that the studio was not operating to its full potential. He recommended that "we pull in our horns a little and produce a limited number of good quality programs." Within the next two years, Jones left the library. David Schroeder, representative of a group called Manna Media, which had been renting the television studio since 1977 for religious programs, observed that no library employee other than Jones had a working knowledge of the studio.

Peters's major achievement while at the Natrona County Public Library was the acquisition of a computer system to conduct the library's circulation functions. He invited a computer firm called Computer Library Services, Inc., to demonstrate its circulation module in September 1978. In May 1979, he convinced the Library Trustees to appropriate $114,000 to purchase the system.

During his four years at the library's helm, he was a strong advocate for the library staff. Within a year of his arrival at the library, he was able to obtain a mid-budget-year 5 percent salary increase for the library staff. He also encouraged the Library Trustees to invite staff representatives to attend the monthly Board meetings. In 1978, he noted that the library had become much busier than in previous years and observed the impact of increased workloads on staff members. In the 1978 annual report to the Wyoming State Library, he wrote, "We have experienced increases in the use of every category of service…without increase in the size of the staff." That resulted in "a lot of people who are tireder at the end of the day." Peters remained the Director until June 23, 1979.

A Brief Tenure

To replace Peters, the Library Trustees hired B. M. "Bob" Desai, who remained at the library for less than a year. While the circumstances of his departure are somewhat unclear, he did not seem to be a good match for the library and apparently failed to meet the performance expectations of library officials. Perhaps the most

B. M. "Bob" Desai served as Library Director for a short term in 1980-81. Photo from NCPL files.

This photo of Frank Schepis, taken in the Director's office, features a clock that appears in various photos throughout the library's history. Although its age and origin are unknown, the earliest photos show it atop the junior department fireplace in the 1925 library addition. This heirloom still runs and may be as old as the library itself.
Photo from NCPL files.

notable act of his short tenure was the formation of an advisory committee to study the Johnson Memorial Studio situation and to make recommendations for its future.

Karen Hill, a member of the studio committee, submitted a memorandum to Desai in May 1980 stating that the studio "lies idle and unused by the library." Shortly after this, Desai left the library. Mary Lynn Corbett, head of the reference department, became the Acting Director while the Board searched for a new director.

A Director from Texas

In early 1981, the Board of Trustees chose Frank Schepis of Weatherford, Texas, to be the library's next Director. Schepis had been the Deputy Director of the Springfield-Green County Library System in Springfield, Missouri. One of his first challenges at the Natrona County Public Library was deciding what to do with the Johnson Memorial Studio. Karen Hill sent a memo to the Library Board members in May 1981 recommending "that the Natrona County Public Library

Susan Haley (center) filled many roles during and after Peters's tenure as Director. Having worked at a variety of library jobs including Resource Specialist in the audiovisual department from 1969 until her retirement in 1987, Haley was best known for her talents as a puppeteer, singer, hostess, and all-around performer.
Photo from NCPL files.

terminate all attempts, by the library or its staff, of any and all programs cable cast from the Johnson Memorial Studio over Cable Channel 12, effective the end of the school year."

A Natrona County School District teacher, Ann Houser, then asked that the school district be allowed to take charge of the studio for classes. The Library Trustees granted the school district the use of the facility for $700 per year. This arrangement, however, proved unsatisfactory to both parties and was terminated on June 1, 1983. Shortly thereafter, the library sold the studio equipment at a silent auction for just over $4,000.

"Old Blue" Bookmobile Rolls In

Soon after his arrival, Schepis presided over a ceremony to dedicate the new bookmobile, dubbed "Old Blue." Since 1980, the Library Trustees had planned to purchase a new vehicle to replace the Reading Roustabout

and received $50,000 for that purpose from a one-cent sales tax. For Old Blue's dedication on July 8, 1981, the Friends of the Library put together a morning of children's activities that featured story time with a real cowgirl and a hobo. Meanwhile, the bookmobile was open for tours throughout the day. The bookmobile was christened with a bottle of champagne by Library Board President Helen Lanning.

Old Blue remained in operation for nearly twenty-five years. The library staff decorated it for events such as the Central Wyoming Fair and Rodeo Parade and the Christmas Light Parade. During an average week, it made approximately twenty stops at rural schools, homebound residences, preschools, day care facilities, and suburban neighborhoods. In 1986, the Homer Truitt Estate gave the library $3,400 for books for Old Blue because of the extensive use Truitt had made of the bookmobile during his lifetime.

"Old Blue" served library patrons for nearly twenty-five years. Driver Cathy Bodenhamer logged many miles behind the wheel.
Photo from NCPL files.

University Ties, the Seventy-Fifth Anniversary, and Improved Budgets

In February 1983, while Schepis was Director, the Library Trustees approved a request from the University of Wyoming to move the university's extension library from Casper College's Goodstein Foundation Library to the public library. The Trustees agreed to let the university house its collection for a period of five years in the basement. On July 13, 1983, the Board approved remodeling the old television studio for the university's use.

Schepis also presided over a ceremony to celebrate the library's seventy-fifth anniversary. To honor this occasion, Schepis had the library purchase special Natrona County Public Library T-shirts, pencils, bookmarks, and mugs. On September 9, 1984, the Friends

Charlotte Babcock, Director Frank Schepis, and Frank Schulte are pictured blowing out the candles on the library's seventy-fifth anniversary "Diamond Jubilee" cake.
Photo from NCPL files.

of the Library hosted an anniversary party featuring a large cake and drinks in honor of two longtime employees, Mildred Morse and Frances Lembeck. An estimated 200 people attended the celebration.

Under Schepis's guidance, budget allocations improved significantly. The first budget of Schepis's tenure, for the 1981-1982 fiscal year, totaled $950,000, an increase of $377,000 from the previous year. The last budget he oversaw, for the 1986-1987 fiscal year, surpassed $1 million for the first time in the library's history.

Requests for a Mills Branch Library

During the tenure of several directors, the Town of Mills submitted requests that the county library establish a branch in Mills. No one in a position of authority, however, did anything to promote or answer the request. In December 1985, Mills officials revisited their request to develop a branch library. At the Library Board meeting on December 12, 1985, Schepis told the Trustees that Mills was "offering a rent-free building in or near the Mills city complex for a branch library." The Board members agreed to consider the proposal once they received a formal letter of request. However, no one acted on behalf of the proposal.

In June 1987, the people of Mills gathered enough donated books to form the nucleus of a lending library. Town officials rewarded this effort by allowing the collection to be housed in a building that had once been the town's carpentry shop and police station. Although this operation had no official ties to the county library in 1987, the new facility stood as a reminder that the citizens of Mills desired to have their own library, just as the people of Casper first expressed their interest in a library by gathering a small collection of books in 1902.

Director Janus Olsen was forced to reduce staff and library hours as county revenues fell.
Photo from NCPL files.

Local Economy Begins to Decline

Frank Schepis submitted his resignation as Director of the Natrona County Public Library in April 1986. He had been so successful at guiding the library that the Trustees asked him to stay. However, he was intent on moving to Seattle, where he became the manager for the Kirkland Library, a branch of the King County Library System. The Trustees began a search for Schepis's replacement and appointed librarian Karling Abernathy to serve as Acting Director.

On August 1, 1986, the Library Trustees hired Janus Olsen of Aberdeen, South Dakota, to be the new administrator. Olsen came to the library at a time when the Natrona County economy was severely declining. The local economy was affected by the closure of two

local banks, reduced local tax revenues, inflation in utility costs, and a slump in the county's oil industry as a result of declining petroleum prices. Whereas Schepis had enjoyed generous budget allocations from the county, Olsen experienced just the opposite. During his first full budget year, Olsen received less than $300,000 in county funds for the library. While his budgets fared better after that first year, reaching nearly $725,000 in 1991, the lack of money seriously affected the library.

Contributions by the Friends of the Library

One source of revenue for the Natrona County Public Library has been the Friends of the Library through the annual spring book

Kathleen Hemry organized and presided over the first Friends of the Library book sale. Other leaders included Wilma Bovie and Betty Ouderkirk, whose combined efforts have resulted in more than thirty-five years of annual sales.
Photo from NCPL files.

sales. The Friends of the Library was organized in 1966 to support a library construction bond issue. In 1972 the Friends began an annual book sale under the guidance of retired Natrona County High School teacher Kathleen Hemry. The first sale, on April 15, 1972, netted $2,100. In 1974, the Friends organization broadened its activities to include an annual meeting and spaghetti dinner that has been held every November since then.

Declared by the Friends the "largest in the Northern Rockies," their book sale has sold tens of thousands of recycled books yearly, including as many as 800 rare books at silent auction. By the early 1990s, the annual event

had become so popular that in 1992 the Friends added a smaller sale of paperback books each autumn. First under the effective guidance of Kathleen Hemry and then through the dedication of Wilma Bovie and Betty Ouderkirk, the Friends book sales began to take in tens of thousand of dollars.

By the time of their twenty-first annual sale in 1992, the Friends had cumulatively given the library nearly $260,000 from their operations since 1972. Their generous contributions added roughly 3 percent to the Natrona County Public Library's annual budget. In addition to donating monies for library book purchases, during the 1980s the Friends had funded a variety of library

Throughout the years, the Friends of the Library book sale posters have touched on a myriad of themes and artistic styles.
Poster created by Zachary Pullen for the Friends of the Library 2000 book sale, from NCPL files.

At one time, the Friends of the Library kept book collection boxes at various points in the community.
Photo by Leon Campbell, published March 16, 1972, in the Casper Star-Tribune. Reprinted with permission.

This photo taken from the roof above the library's south entrance shows the crowd waiting to enter the Friends of the Library book sale in 1986.
Photo from NCPL files.

projects, such as a protective, weather-resistant coat for the Prometheus statue in 1981, an automatic sliding door at the parking lot entrance to the library in 1985, and books for the Edgerton Branch and the bookmobile in 1988.

Hard Times Begin

As early as 1935, poor funding levels had been a problem for the county library. During Olsen's tenure, funding was constantly a challenge. In January 2007, Trula Cooper, Pinky Ellis, and Art Volk recalled some of their experiences as Library Trustees in the 1970s. One challenge they all remembered was obtaining adequate funding for the library. A decade after their terms, this situation became acute. In February 1987, in keeping with the region's economic

woes, the Trustees expressed a need to prepare for what they termed a "reduced economy." That year budgetary setbacks forced the library to close on Sundays. Shortly thereafter, the library downsized its staff from sixty-seven employees to fifty-four because of a 15 percent reduction in the operating budget. Sensing the results of such cuts, Board members affirmed on July 29, 1987, the "importance of a well trained, adequate staff to serve library patrons." Within a year, however, the Board faced the need to cut another $40,000 from the budget. Instead of cutting staff this time, library officials decided to spread much of this decrease over the various collections. Olsen recommended that "the book budget be cut before jobs or the library's hours."

The Director could accept the reduction of county-allocated monies spent on collection development because other revenue sources had become available for books. These other funds included the one-cent sales tax and Friends of the Library grants from book sale profits. In 1986, the library began to request a share of the county's optional one-cent tax to purchase books and supplies. At the October 10, 1989, Board meeting, the Library Trustees acknowledged that the organization's regular budget plus the one-cent funds was adequate for the library's acquisitions.

Spotlight: 1990
Natrona County Population: 61,200
Casper Population: 46,800

Natrona County Public Library Facts
Library Director: Janus Olsen
Library Collection: 284,100
Circulation: 446,400
Budget: $721,200
Board Members: Sandra Dow, Agnes
   Hand, Marilyn Lyle, Patrick M.
   McDonald, J. M. Neil, Joe Sabel

Despite receiving one-cent sales tax monies and Friends donations, the county library continued to experience difficult financial times into the 1990s. At the April 1991 Board meeting, the Library Trustees authorized the Director to cut the library's hours of operation and reduce the staff by five people. In 1992, library employees offered to take furloughs in response to a budget cut. In June of that year, the library suffered a 35 percent budget reduction when the County Commissioners cut $220,000 from the library's 1992-1993 budget year request for $815,000. To meet this drastic downturn, the Board reduced Olsen's salary by 10 percent and cut the library staff by several people. Then it reduced library hours to a scant forty per week: 11:00 a.m. to 7:00 p.m. Monday through Thursday and 1:00 to 5:00 p.m. Friday and Saturday. It also shifted all book purchases to one-cent monies. Greta Lehnerz, the library's administrative assistant and bookkeeper, said, "This was an awful day for everyone."

Book Theft: Ever a Problem

Adding to the library's budget woes of the 1980s and early 1990s was the news that a frequent problem had resurfaced: the loss through theft of library materials. There had already been signs of this problem when, in 1982, Frank Schepis informed the Board that magazines were being stolen. In 1985, he again announced that large numbers of books were being stolen. The problem did not go away. On December 8, 1987, Karling Abernathy, head of the library's book selection committee, told the Board that her committee members were "making book selections based on what is going to be stolen so the committee is requesting that some sort of security system be put into the library." Technical processing department head Beverly Diehl added, "Based on an inventory done, approximately $88,000 worth of books have been stolen in the Adult Nonfiction category alone since 1977." To combat theft, the library installed a security system in 1990.

Another Leadership Transition

Amid these changes, Janus Olsen had to undergo serious surgery, for which he took 60 days of medical leave starting in November 1991. Joan Hoff, librarian at the Edgerton Branch, became the Director pro tem during Olsen's absence. Olsen submitted a letter of resignation with an effective date of September 21, 1992. Accepting his letter, the Board appointed Greta Lehnerz as the library's Acting Director until it could find a replacement for Olsen. Despite the continued cycle of change, Olsen's departure gave the Trustees an opportunity to hire someone with a fresh outlook on the library's future potential. Their decision would prove to be a good one.

Summary

Moving toward the end of the twentieth century, Natrona County underwent many changes. The Natrona County Public Library did as well. The library purchased a new bookmobile, experimented with fresh technologies, and experienced a number of leadership changes, as directors came and went with more frequency than before. The 1970s brought a new library building, a branch in Edgerton, and a new bookmobile, as well as the Friends of the Library book sale to help raise funds. In 1984, the library celebrated its seventy-fifth anniversary. Although Natrona County experienced increased growth in the early 1970s, the economy began to slow in the late 1980s, leading to budget cuts at the library. A new director would soon evaluate these improvements and hardships. That director would need to encourage new direction and renewed commitment to service in order for the library to remain relevant to the community.

Chapter Six: A Story that Never Ends

1993-2010

*Few resources in our community are more valuable
than a quality, modern library.*

John Masterson, Natrona County Public Library Foundation President, 2006-Present

Natrona County was still in an economic slump in 1992, when the Library Board of Trustees convened to find a library director to replace Janus Olsen. The nearly eighty-year-old Amoco Oil Refinery on the west side of town had shut down and the region's first railroad, the Chicago & North Western, would soon cease to serve the area. Library budgets would fluctuate but remained below the pinnacle they had reached under Frank Schepis's directorship. Yet the library was on firm foundations. Its Board, directors, and staff had taken good care of the main facility, maintained a branch in Edgerton and bookmobile service throughout the county, received one-cent sales tax support, and been given financial and public relations assistance from the Friends of the Library.

In early 1993, the Trustees chose Lesley D. Boughton as the library's twelfth Director. Boughton was well acquainted with Wyoming's public libraries. At the time of her selection, she was the head of the Carbon County Library, and before that she had been the Director of the Platte County Library. With a master's degree in library science from Southern Connecticut State University, her background was excellent for the job.

One of Boughton's early challenges upon arriving at the Natrona County Public Library was to expand the library's hours to include Sundays. The County Commissioners' library liaison, Marion Bouzis, had several times requested Sunday hours, and Boughton was able to comply with his request. On August 10, 1993, Boughton announced to the Board that the library would be open from 1:00 to 6:00 p.m. on Sundays from October through May. Even in the face of a budget cut in 1995, she kept the Sunday hours, only reducing them to 1:00 to 5:00 p.m.

As Director, Lesley Boughton oversaw NCPL's connection to the Internet and statewide electronic resources.
Photo from NCPL files.

The Wyoming Library Database

One of Boughton's more salient actions was to connect the library to the statewide computer system known as WyLD (Wyoming Library Database) in 1992, which replaced the antiquated card catalog. For the previous two years, the library had been using a statewide computerized system operated by the GEAC Corporation, which offered circulation, card catalog, reference, and interlibrary capabilities. On October 13, 1992, Library Board President Dick Jay signed an agreement with the Wyoming State Library to link the Natrona County Public Library to WyLD. This gave staff and patrons increased access to library holdings across the state.

On July 13, 1995, the *Casper Star-Tribune* reported that the old card catalog was gone and that by early 1996, the main facility would have thirty computer terminals linked to WyLD. The Library Board minutes for October 12, 1995, stated that the former card catalog would be auctioned in November.

Building-Wide Renovations

Boughton's greatest accomplishment during her time at the Natrona County Public Library was a building renovation program. This program consisted of using financial grants from the federal government and local one-cent taxes to rearrange the main and second floor collections and to remodel the basement for a new children's department. Specifically, she planned to remodel the former Johnson Memorial Studio in the basement for the children's department, and then move the information services department (including the reference desk, adult nonfiction, federal documents, petroleum collection, and a new Patent and Trademark Depository Library) to the second floor.

Following the completion of these projects, Boughton oversaw the remodeling of the first floor to make it compliant with the Americans with Disabilities Act, improve the efficiency of the checkout area, and provide more attractive space for the fiction collection. The project cost approximately $650,000, with $72,000 coming from the Friends of the Library, approximately $500,000 from optional one-cent taxes, and approximately $80,000 from a federal Library Services and Technology Act grant. Of this project, the *Casper Star-Tribune* stated on June 18, 1997, "The redesign will allow for better

TRICIA McINROY/STAR-TRIBUNE

Library Trustees Doug Morton, left, and Doug Cooper cart away a card catalog as maintenance head Vernon Boyce observes.
Photo by Tricia McInroy, **Casper Star-Tribune***, November 13, 1995.*
Reprinted with permission.

use of existing space in the building…and will [in Boughton's words] 'provide a quiet floor for study space.'"

One of the most attractive portions of the renovation project was the children's department. Once it was finished, Boughton wrote to Christine N. Brady, a colleague from Boise, Idaho, to describe her progress in detail. "I am happy to let you [know]," she wrote, "that we have achieved our objective of building a new children's library as the first phase of our building program." She then explained how she had obtained funding for the new area. "I made a successful presentation to the citizen's committee which determines allocation of the optional one-cent sales tax which is on the ballot every four years. We received $257,000 which we used for the children's library."

When the children's department, information services department, and fiction area were complete, Boughton held a grand opening to showcase the project that had been the focus of a great deal of her time and energy. The celebration took place on December 18, 1998, highlighting the newly created children's room.

Mills Library Becomes an Official NCPL Branch

Another advancement that occurred during Boughton's administration was the formalization of ties between the county library and the Mills library. In December 1997, the Natrona County Commissioners signed a memorandum of understanding with Mills officials that the Natrona County Public Library would begin operating the Mills facility on a reimbursable basis. In early 1998, the Town of Mills agreed to pay the county $15,000 to reimburse the cost of operating the Mills Branch Library for that year. The branch then reopened as part of the county library system.

In July 2003, the Mills Town Council renamed their branch library the Bob Goff Memorial Library in honor of their recently deceased Mayor who had labored diligently to secure the library in Mills. In 2004, Mills received a grant from the Natrona County Recreation Joint Powers Board to provide a 1,400-square-foot addition to the library building. The expanded facility was opened in October 2005, operating under a new agreement between the Town of Mills and the Library Trustees.

The Bob Goff Memorial Library in Mills was expanded in 2005. Photo from NCPL files.

New Leadership for the Library

On December 31, 1998, shortly after the library held its open house to showcase its recent renovations, Boughton left to become the Wyoming State Librarian. The Natrona County Public Library Trustees designated Jerry Jones, Youth Services Coordinator, as the Acting Director and then formed a search committee to begin the process of finding another director. This committee consisted of Lynnette Anderson (Casper College librarian), Ruth Adelman (Library Trustee from 1992 to 1995), and Doug Cooper (Library Trustee from 1995 to 2001). The committee recommended, and the Trustees selected, Bill Nelson, a librarian, graduate of the United States Naval Academy, and career officer in the Navy's Civil Engineer Corps.

Coming from the state of Washington, Nelson was well versed in librarianship, having worked in the Microsoft Corporation Library and

Since becoming Director of NCPL in 1999, Bill Nelson has emphasized staff teamwork and community engagement.
Photo from NCPL files.

earning a master's degree in Library and Information Science from the University of Washington. After graduate school, Nelson worked at both Washington's multiple-branch King County and Sno-Isle Regional Library Systems. Having honed his leadership skills through his experience in the Navy and at several Washington libraries, Nelson came to Casper well prepared to take charge of the Natrona County Public Library.

Barbara Bush Reading Room

Before leaving the Natrona County Public Library, Boughton had laid the groundwork for the creation of a special library room called the Barbara Bush Reading Room. When completed, the room occupied a remodeled alcove on the library's first floor and housed materials from a ten-year-old section called the Adult Learning Center. The Casper Republican women's organization funded the Barbara Bush Room in late 1997, but the library did not finish working on the room until mid-1999.

It fell to Nelson to arrange a dedication celebration to coincide with National Family Literacy Day on November 1, 1999. Guests included County Commission liaison to the library Cathy Killean, Natrona County Public Library Board of Trustees President Doug Cooper, Natrona County Republican Party President Rosa Goolsby, and community literacy and education volunteers Lisa Mixer and Julie Eastes.

James Crawford Honored

In June 2000, Nelson had the honor of nominating and later announcing that former Library Trustee James G. Crawford had received an American Library Association award for being one of Wyoming's five extraordinary library advocates of the twentieth century. In a June 5, 2000, news release, Nelson stated, "Mr. Crawford is best remembered for his leadership in expanding library facilities. In 1967, he coordinated a bond issue to purchase additional

The library's public meeting room was named for former Trustee James G. Crawford.
Photo from NCPL files.

Building Community

Upon arriving in Casper in early June 1999, Nelson became extremely energetic in improving library budgets, enhancing programs and community outreach, and re-adjusting book collections and space arrangements within the library. As quoted in the *Casper Star-Tribune* on October 3, 1999, the new Director stated that he wanted to create a library "that is relevant and helps everyone in the community." Nelson encouraged the dynamic expansion of library activities because of his focus on involving the library in the life of its community. "Libraries build communities," Nelson wrote in *Community Builder*, a Natrona County Public Library newsletter he initiated. The title reflected Nelson's emphasis on making the library an integral part of the county's life.

Nelson and Trustee Cary Brus planned a leadership reception for January 30, 2001, to raise community awareness about the library's poor funding situation. Fifty community leaders attended the reception hosted by Mick and Susie McMurry of the McMurry Foundation. At the reception, Nelson and Board President Doug Cooper emphasized the need for raising awareness that the Natrona County Public Library was, on a per capita basis, the least-funded

land, expand the library facilities, purchase a bookmobile, and to improve the facilities at the Midwest/Edgerton branch."

After the 1967 bond proposal failed to win voter approval, Crawford persisted in pursuing funding for a new library until voters finally passed a bond issue in August 1969. Nelson wrote, "The improvements that he envisioned were realized in 1972, the same year that he passed away. To honor Mr. Crawford's strong leadership in building and equipping the library, a Community Room was named in his honor." Nelson concluded, "A plaque honoring Jim as an 'extraordinary library advocate of the 20th century' will be hung in the Crawford Room." The American Library Association honored Crawford at its annual conference in Chicago in July 2000, and the Wyoming Library Association paid tribute to him at its conference in Riverton, Wyoming, on September 21.

Spotlight: 2000
Natrona County Population: 66,500
Casper Population: 49,600

Natrona County Public Library Facts
Library Director: Bill Nelson
Library Collection: 204,000
Circulation: 338,900
Budget: $827,900
Board Members: Ray Bader, Jennifer Black, Cary Brus, Doug Cooper, Wendy Rilett

public library in Wyoming and one of the poorest in the nation. The library suffered from such chronically low budgets that it was unable to properly serve county citizens. Nelson felt confident that the leadership reception provided a major turning point toward improved financial support for the public library because civic leaders were now aware of the situation.

Tackling the challenges of improving the library's funding and operations, Nelson convened a strategic planning session in November 2002 with the Library Trustees to discuss long-range library goals. A central theme that emerged from this meeting was the library's importance to the community it serves.

The Director and the Board recognized the need for the library to receive adequate and stable funding. As a means to achieve that goal, they believed it was necessary to improve public relations, raising awareness of the value the library provides.

Raising Funds for the Library

Emphasizing the library's active role in community affairs, Nelson successfully acquired the funds needed to expand collections, outreach programs, and facilities. His first budget request, for the 2001 fiscal year, netted the library a gain of approximately $60,000 from the last budget of his predecessor. In 2001 the County

The Friends of the Library made a major contribution to fuel the NCPL Foundation's first fund-raising campaign.
Top row: Pamela Reamer-Williams, Bill Thompson, Doug Morton, Nancy Witzeling. Bottom row: Cary Brus, Drew
Walker, Wilma Bovie, Joy Mascarenas, Betty Ouderkirk, Sally Bailey.
Photo from NCPL files.

Commissioners approved the Board's 2002 budget request for $1 million. This was the first time the library had received that much money since 1986, when Frank Schepis was the Director. By the summer of 2009, the library budget had risen to $2.6 million.

Nelson has been adroit at networking with the county and the state to acquire funds for the library. In 2002, the library received $225,000 annually for two years because of the efforts of Nick Murdock, a Casper attorney. Murdock was instrumental in creating the Natrona County Recreation Joint Powers Board to support professional development for Natrona County School District #1 teachers. The funds from the Joint Powers Board allowed Nelson to hire additional library staff and offer more programs. Nelson has continued to nurture relationships with Joint Powers Board officials, ensuring ongoing financial support from that Board. Recently, the library received a $24,000 grant for the 2010 summer reading program. The library's interaction with the Joint Powers Board emphasizes, in Nelson's words, the value of a "meaningful partnership between government and lifelong learning institutions like the library."

Another example of working within the community to secure adequate funding is the expansion of the Natrona County Public Library Foundation's role in fund-raising activities. The Foundation was formed in 1972 to receive private donations made to the library. During the summer of 2000, Nick Murdock assisted Nelson and former Trustee Doug Morton by amending the Natrona County Public Library Foundation's Articles of Incorporation to make it an agency independent of the Library Board of Trustees.

In 2002, the Foundation began its first fund-raising campaign, "A Story that Never Ends," with a goal of $250,000. In March 2002, the Friends of the Library donated $100,000 of

Friends of the Library Board 2010

Robin Broumley
Jean Fenner
Laurie Fletcher
Barb Gurkin
Bob Hopkins
Dorothy Hulett
Pat Johnson
Larry Linn
David Long
Joy Mascarenas
Chris Mullen – President
Donna Mullen
Betty Ouderkirk
Nancy Witzeling

accumulated funds toward the Foundation's goal. Upon reaching the goal of this first campaign, the Foundation began a second phase called "Over the Top!" with a goal of $1 million, reached successfully in 2008.

Nelson also played a key role in creating a funding initiative called the Public Library Endowment Challenge Program, which the Wyoming Library Association carried to the State Legislature in 2008. Nelson met with Wyoming Governor Dave Freudenthal and the Natrona County legislative delegation in late 2007 to encourage their support of the concept. When it was introduced in the 2008 Wyoming Senate, it became known as Senate Bill 29. The bill provided the opportunity for the state's public libraries to acquire and save funds during a time of prosperity and encouraged them to develop fundraising skills. Nelson announced to the Library Board on March 6, 2008, that this endowment program had been signed into law. According to the legislation, the state will give each Wyoming county library foundation state funds to match the endowment monies it raises. The amount of money received depends on the total county valuation. The economically strongest counties have a one-to-one match, mid-range counties two-to-one, and the poorest counties three-to-one. The Natrona County Public Library has the opportunity to earn approximately $295,000 over a five-year period for participating in this state endowment program.

Overall, Nelson's success in obtaining additional funding for the Natrona County Public Library has been phenomenal. In March 2009, Jackie Read, a member of the Board of Trustees that hired Nelson, stated that he "has performed miracles with fundraising."

Enhanced Library Collections

Updating the library's book collections was one of Nelson's earliest goals. In 2000, he announced in the library's annual report that for the first time in many years the library staff had initiated a comprehensive removal of outdated, dilapidated, or otherwise unused items from the library's collection. On October 11, 2006, the *Casper Star-Tribune* reported that nearly 50,000 "old, tattered and beat-up" books had been removed from the library. Once this was completed in 2001, Nelson turned his attention to adding books with more current content. In 2003, the average publication date of a book in the library was 1972; by 2006, the average date was 1986. While upgrading the book collection, staff members also began to acquire more diverse types of materials such as DVDs and CDs.

As an integral part of making the library's collection more current and relevant to patrons' needs, Nelson began to downsize collections that no longer served the public. One collection that the Director decided to decrease was federal documents. In a letter to a United States Government Printing Office

official in September 2004, Nelson explained the necessity of eliminating the majority of the government documents so that the materials remaining in the library would consist of "those very few items of benefit to our community." In addition, Nelson sent all of the county library's patent and trademark documents to the Wyoming State Library.

Nelson also fine-tuned and relocated the Wyoming collection, which had been on the library mezzanine since the late 1960s. He accomplished this by having library employees identify the unique and valuable Wyoming books and transferring those materials to two specially remodeled alcoves on the second floor. This remodeling cost $27,000 and was completed in the autumn of 2003. As part of redefining this collection, library staff transferred the majority of the commonly available Wyoming-related books to the general stacks.

A Colorful New Bookmobile

In 2003, the Library Board of Trustees approved the replacement of the 1981 bookmobile, Old Blue, with a new vehicle. Using $188,000 of optional one-cent tax money for the bookmobile and $14,700 from the Friends of the Library for exterior graphics, the library bought a model from Matthew's Specialty Vehicles of Greensboro, North Carolina. The creation of an exterior design to reflect Wyoming's unique heritage brought community interest and involvement. Local artist Chris Navarro created the overall concept and Board member Chris Mullen arranged historical icons and petroglyphs. Nancy Witzeling of the Friends of the Library also served on the design committee. Bob Treick of Wit's End Photography took the photo of Casper Mountain, which serves as the background of the design.

The new bookmobile made its debut at a ribbon-cutting ceremony on July 7, 2004. As an extension of the library's outreach efforts,

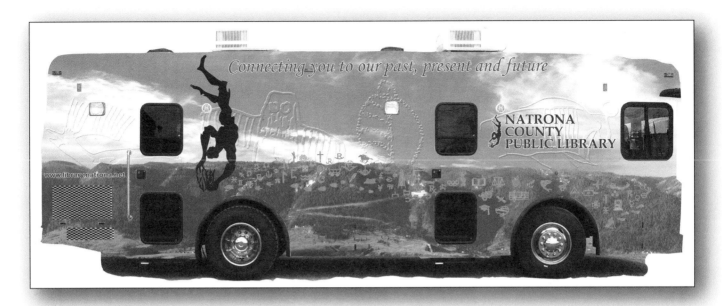

The current bookmobile continues an outreach tradition, covered with designs reflecting our community and its history. Photo from NCPL files.

the vehicle has participated in community events such as the Central Wyoming Fair and Rodeo Parade, the annual Christmas Light Parade, the 2007 "Tina's Drive for Life" blood drive, and the Beartrap Summer Festival. It makes regular stops at over fifty locations, including Alcova, Bar Nunn, the Casper Recreation Center, Evansville, Mountain View, Paradise Valley, Poison Spider, Powder River, Vista Hills, and Wolf Creek.

Teen Zone and Technology Center

Moving the Wyoming collection allowed Nelson to initiate several building renovations. With the old mezzanine available for other uses, he created a team of library staff and young people from the community to design a "teen zone" to occupy the mezzanine. The team selected color schemes, funky furniture, and special shelving to give the new area a teen-friendly atmosphere. Nelson then had a portion of the mezzanine remodeled using monies from the Friends of the Library, one-cent sales taxes, the Recreation Joint Powers Board, and the Tate, Tonkin, and Daniel Foundations.

While creating the Teen Zone, Nelson and his staff laid plans to establish a technology center on the first floor. A Natrona County Public Library Foundation report stated,

The former "problem" area on the mezzanine was transformed into a multipurpose Teen Zone. Photo from NCPL files.

"The Tech Center will be a community-focused program providing the public with free access to frontline technology with the best internet available." The Tech Center was built simultaneously under the same contract with the Teen Zone. When finished, the Tech Center featured sixteen computers for public use. The library held a joint grand opening on February 1, 2005, to celebrate the completion of both the Teen Zone and the Tech Center.

Community-Centered Programs and Outreach

Keeping with his philosophy of making the Natrona County Public Library relevant to its community, Nelson expanded the library's operations to incorporate a number of new programs. The offerings included book discussions, art exhibits, musical performances, computer classes, storytime, classroom tours, and author visits, as well as programs specifically for families, teens, children, and seniors.

In 2000, the library joined with John Jorgensen in an annual event called "Casper Cares, Casper Reads" that he created to honor his late wife. The Sue Jorgensen Library Foundation produces this annual event, at which every local first-grade student receives a quality hardback book. The program became so popular that it expanded in 2006 to become "Wyoming Reads" and now provides hardback books to more than 7,200 first-graders throughout Wyoming. In addition to giving each first-grade student a book, the event features a storytime session with local celebrities, a special lunch, and a dramatization of a fairy tale about the Good Queen Sue.

The Natrona County Public Library started a program called "Teen Poetry Slam" in 2001. This event featured local young people reading their original poetry at a talent show sponsored by the library and held in a local coffee house. Each participant would read three poems in front of a group of judges and an audience. The poetry slam was designed to enhance teens' self-confidence and create a sense of literary community reminiscent of the 1950s beat poetry movement.

In 2007, library staff began an outreach program to serve patrons who are unable to visit the library due to a temporary or long-term physical or mental disability, as well as their caregivers. Through Books By Mail, the library sends books, DVDs, audiobooks, and other materials to patrons' homes. Postage is paid both ways, and Books By Mail patrons do not accrue late fees.

The summer reading program and storytime are good examples of the library's expanded offerings for children. From 500 participants in 1973, summer reading has grown exponentially. In 2009, participants included 2,700 children, 580 teens, and 1,400 adults. Storytime has been equally successful. The library's 2009 annual report listed more than 200 storytime programs held at the main library and the Mills Branch, attracting 5,500 children and adults.

The library also participated in an annual reading program for adults called "One Book, One Community." The program began with "Everybody Reads Mark Spragg" in 2004. Participants have also read *To Kill a Mockingbird* by Harper Lee and *Pay It Forward* by Catherine Ryan Hyde.

Reminiscent of the Bookworm program of the 1950s and 1960s, the library has participated with the Natrona County School District #1 in a project called "Reading Is Fundamental" since the late 1970s. The program involves library staff members making three visits a year to as many as sixteen Casper area schools in order to distribute books to approximately 1,000 at-risk students in the second and fifth grades. Local funding for Reading Is Fundamental comes from the Friends of the Library.

Local television news anchor Alex Haight participates as a celebrity reader in the NCPL children's department during the 2009 Wyoming Reads celebration.
Photo from NCPL files.

Another program organized by local schools and the library is the spring Elementary Art Show. Since 1999, the library has collaborated with the Natrona County School District #1 in showcasing up to 13,000 individual pieces of student artwork. Each student in kindergarten through sixth grade has at least one piece of art displayed at the library for several weeks each spring. A reception kicks off each year's event. Maps are available to guide parents and visitors through the displays, which include painting, sculpture, mixed media, collage, and watercolor.

While this is only a small sample of the many activities the Natrona County Public Library has created to connect with the community, the annual reports give much more detailed information on library activities and short- and long-term goals. For example, the 2009 annual report (Appendix Four) highlights in more detail the programs and outreach for children, teens, tweens, and adults, as well as community involvement, grants and awards, technology use, and circulation statistics. The library collaborated with Boys and Girls Club, Head Start, and the Juvenile Detention Center, and took part in the Natrona County School District's Back to School Bash, the Wyoming Women's Expo, the Platte River Parkway Fall Festival, and many other events.

Each spring, the library's three floors are filled with art created by Natrona County elementary school students. The Elementary Art Show reception features crafts like those shown here and provides an opportunity for community members, families, and friends to view each child's masterpiece.
Photo from NCPL files.

The Beginning of a New Era for the Library

Statistically, the Natrona County Public Library was better off in 2009 than it had ever been in its nearly one hundred year history. According to the 2009 annual report, circulation numbers soared to a record-breaking 630,900 items. Patrons made 368,900 visits to the library. Library employees added more than 21,000 items to the collection from July 1, 2008, through June 30, 2009.

The library's sources of revenue have been expanded through the efforts and contributions of the Friends, Foundation, one-cent sales taxes, and the Natrona County Recreation Joint Powers Board. Additionally, the Foundation has raised more than $295,000 to meet its state match under the Public Library Endowment Challenge Program.

Voting for a New Library Facility

Despite the impressive statistics, the library is facing a major obstacle to the further expansion of services: the limitations of the main library's physical facility. As of July 2009, the building contained 32,000 square feet. When the Library

Trustees planned the 1972 replacement of the original Carnegie building, they did so believing that once construction was completed, the library would have sufficient space to last twenty-five years.

By 2006, library officials realized that the space of the two wings had become inadequate for the library's future needs.

A great amount of effort was put into planning for a new library facility. In 2006, the Library Director and Trustees created a strategic plan that recognized the need for a larger library. In 2007, the Board formed a site selection committee consisting of Trustees and local citizens. After conferring with County Commissioners in early 2008, the Board hired an architectural team to assist with such details as defining space needs, conducting site evaluations, putting together financial details, and creating floor plans and concept diagrams. In addition to planning the new facility, the Library Board considered what might be done with the current library. While planning moved forward, several citizens organized a committee called Citizens for a New Library.

A key element of the new library plan was the acquisition of an 8.8-acre piece of property in the Old Yellowstone District along West First Street. The purchase of this land would give the county library an opportunity to construct a building large enough for an expanded children's department, more public meeting rooms, and enlarged facilities for more technological resources. It would also allow the library to provide additional, much-needed parking.

This architect's drawing by Burnidge Cassell Associates depicts the entrance for the new library building proposed to the public in 2008.
Illustration from NCPL files.

In 2008, the Library Trustees announced a plan to acquire the new site for the library at a cost of $3.8 million. On that 8.8-acre site would be built a 96,000-square-foot structure that would last, in the opinion of one supporter, "at least another 40 years." To fund the new plan, library officials asked Natrona County voters to approve a temporary one-cent sales tax increase to obtain $43.25 million. Overall, this library proposal would, in the language of the election ballot, "expand literacy, education, programs and services for all citizens."

While those leading the expansion program explained the need for a new library facility on a new site, the ballot proposal generated controversy within the county. Debate swirled around two key issues: the price of $3.8 million for a parcel of land and the need for a 96,000-square-foot building.

When the project came to a vote on November 4, 2008, the library's request failed by a vote of 17,132 against and 15,578 in favor. This was the second time in the library's history that voters rejected paying additional taxes to support a building project. The first time was in 1967, two years before Natrona County voters approved the 1969 library construction proposal.

After the Election

On November 6, 2008, a *Casper Star-Tribune* editorial advised, "The size of the new library needs to be studied.... A more modest increase might be more palatable to voters." Regarding the purchase of the Old Yellowstone District site, the editorial noted, "Some people questioned the approximately $3.8 million purchase price of the land.... But as the assessor's office and local Realtors tried to explain, the cost per square foot was in line with other commercial property in the area." Above all, the *Star-Tribune* opinion piece encouraged, "Library supporters shouldn't give up; there will be time to revisit the issue."

That is a statement worth remembering. Library officials did not give up in 1967 when voters elected not to approve a library bond issue. The project came back to a vote in 1969 and passed.

On November 6, 2008, two days following the election, Mick and Susie McMurry gave a $1 million donation to the Natrona County Public Library Foundation. As quoted in the December 2008 issue of *Community Builder*, "The McMurrys wished to express their confidence in the library's value to our community."

Land Acquisition

Within a year of the library's failed 2008 sales tax ballot initiative, the Natrona County Public Library Foundation had raised enough money to purchase a 5.4-acre piece of property in the Old Yellowstone District. The Foundation purchased the property from the Casper Redevelopment Company and JBC Investments. John Masterson, President of the Foundation, stated that the action has "no downside." An article in the *Casper Journal*

Mick and Susie McMurry supported the NCPL Foundation with a $1 million donation in November 2008. Members of the Board of Trustees and Foundation accept the McMurry's generous gift. Pictured left to right: Foundation President John Masterson, Mick McMurry, Trustee Charles Robertson, Susie McMurry, Trustee President Chris Mullen, Trustee Mary Ann Collins, Foundation member Ray Bader, Director Bill Nelson, Foundation members Mark Zaback, Jimmy Goolsby and Bill Thompson.
Photo by Shannon Wolz from NCPL files.

on November 4, 2009, added, "The property purchase paves the way for going back to the voters sometime in the future for support for construction on the donated site." Regarding a future library, Masterson said, "The need is still there."

The Ongoing Story

Bill Nelson rekindled his spirits almost immediately after the 2008 election. On November 7, 2008, he wrote "Thoughts for the Next Election," a document reflecting on and analyzing the way the county library developed its election campaign. He acknowledged the need to convince the community that the library has outgrown its current facility. During its one hundred year history, the library has been continually renovated and repurposed. Through all the changes, library employees

have demonstrated flexibility and pride in their workplace, as well as a desire to serve the public. The library's history has been a chronicle of fluctuations. Directors and staff

Spotlight: 2010
Natrona County Population: 73,100
Casper Population: 52,100

Natrona County Public Library Facts
Library Director: Bill Nelson
Library Collection: 192,200
Circulation: 630,900
Budget: $2.6 million
Board Members: Randy Buffington,
    Mary Ann Collins, Shawn
    Houck, Harper Lee Park, Charles
    Robertson

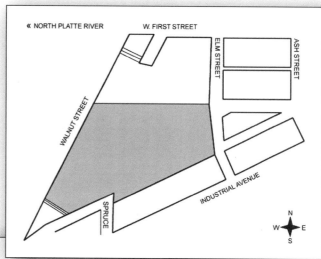

Library Foundation President John Masterson, left, and Board of Trustees President Charles Robertson stand on the former American Pipeyard property in downtown Casper. The Library Foundation purchased the property with private donations as a potential future library site.
Photo by Dale Bohren, Casper Journal, November 4, 2009, reprinted with permission. Property map from NCPL files.

have worked diligently to seek improvement, react to challenges, and enhance the library's value to the community. To borrow the title of the Natrona County Public Library Foundation's first fund-raising effort, the library's history is "a story that never ends."

Nelson and his Board have envisioned a new library in a new location, a library with more to offer its patrons. Theirs is the kind of vision that enabled Wilson S. Kimball to ask Andrew Carnegie in 1905 for funds to build a library for Natrona County. It is the kind of vision that animated LaFrances Sullivan to regroup after the 1967 bond election failure. It is the kind of vision that encouraged Mick and Susie McMurry to support the library's proposed expansion in 2008. The county is now better off for the tenaciousness of these visionaries. Nelson's "Thoughts for the Next Election" is only a preamble to the writing of the next chapter of a story that seems to be without end.

Appendix One:
Natrona County Public Library Trustees

Note: Originally, between 1909 and 1967, the Board consisted of three members. In April 1967, the Board increased to four members. In March 1968, the Board increased to five members.

John E. Schulte, 1909-1918
Charles H. Townsend, 1909-1927
Charles C. P. Webel, 1909
Harold Banner, 1909-1913
J. W. "Billy" Johnson, 1918-1965
May Hamilton, 1921-1927
Joe P. Jacobs, 1927-1928
Carl F. Shumaker, 1927-1945
Philip. K. Edwards, 1929-1933
M. A. Robertson, 1933-1935
Ray O. Taylor, 1935-1938
Nell Kimball, 1938-1943
Thomas Spears, 1943-1947 (died while President of the Board, replaced by Crawford)
Charles L. Rose, 1947-1967
James G. Crawford, 1947-1957 and 1965-1971
Stella Russell (Dunn), 1957-1965: [1947-1961 (Russell), 1961-1965 (Dunn)]
Wanda Walters, 1966-1969
John P. Albanese, 1967-1974 and 1974-1981 (added as a fourth member with Bowron)
Frank L. Bowron, 1967-1972 (added as a fourth member)
Lois Shickich, 1968-1974 (added as a fifth member)
Nona Muller, 1970-1975
Trula Cooper, 1972-1977
Arthur C. Volk, Jr., 1973-1979
Frank J. Ellis, Jr., 1973-1979
Mark J. Davis, Jr., 1974-1978
Sharon Nichols, 1977-1983
Gerald Kennedy, 1979-1982

Helen Lanning, 1979-1983
Mary Masterson, 1979-1985
Donald Swanton, 1981-1987
Murray Dahill, 1982-1989
Harold Meier, 1983-1988
Leigh Flack, 1983-1989
Marilyn Lyle, 1985-1991
Agnes Hand, 1987-1993
J. M. Neil, 1988-1990
Patrick M. McDonald, 1988-1994
Sandra Dow, 1989-1995
Joe Sabel, 1990-1992
Dick Jay, 1991-1995
Ruth Adelman, 1992-1995
Jackie Lynn Read, 1993-1999
Doug Morton, 1994-2000
Doug Cooper, 1995-2001
Scott Burnworth, 1995-1996
Jeanette Miller, 1995-1999
Cary Brus, 1996-2003
Jennifer Black, 1999-2001
Wendy Rilett, 1999-2002
Ray Bader, 2000-2006
Rita Walsh, 2001-2007
Pamela Reamer Williams, 2001-2007
Vickie Cawthra, 2002-2008
Chris Mullen, 2003-2009
Charles Robertson, 2006-
Randy Buffington, 2007-
Mary Ann Collins, 2007-
Harper Lee Park, 2008-
Shawn Houck, 2009-

Appendix Two:
Head Librarians and Directors

Sarah E. Place, May 20-1910 – April 16, 1919

Wilma Shaffner, April 1919 – May 1919 (Acting Librarian)

Effie Cummings Rodgers, June 1, 1919 – June 16, 1927

Elva Randa, June 1927 – March 1928 (Acting Librarian)

Eleanor Davis, April 1928 – September 1937

Genevra Brock, September 15, 1937 – April 1943

Margaret Burke, April 1943 – October 1957

LaFrances McCoy Sullivan, October 1957 – August 1969

Mildred Morse, April 1969 – November 1969 (Acting Librarian)

Kenneth Dowlin, December 1969 – March 1975

Elizabeth Fuller, March 1975 – August 1975 (Acting Director)

John Peters, September 1975 – June 1979

B. M. "Bob" Desai, August 1979 – July 1980

Mary Lynn Corbett, August 1980 – March 1981 (Acting Director)

Frank Schepis, March 1981 – April 18, 1986

Karling Abernathy, April 19, 1986 – July 1986 (Acting Director)

Janus Olsen, August 1, 1986 – September 4, 1992

Joan Hoff, November – December 1991 (Director pro tem)

Greta Lehnerz, September 1992 – May 1993 (Acting Director)

Lesley D. Boughton, May 1, 1993 – December 31, 1998

Jerry Jones, January 1999 – May 1999 (Acting Director)

Bill Nelson, June 1, 1999 – Present

Appendix Three:
Recognition Awards
(Individuals or groups associated with the Natrona County Public Library)

To all those recognized over the years and to all those who have worked in Wyoming libraries we collectively say, "You are all winners."

Wyoming Library Association

American Library Association/Association of Library Trustees and Advocates

James G. Crawford: "Extraordinary Library Advocate of the 20th Century," 2000

Mountain Plains Library Association

Natrona County Recreation Joint Powers Board: Legislative Leadership Award, 2003

Wyoming Library Association

Chris Mullen: Trustee Citation, 2009

Mick and Susie McMurry: Meritorious Service Award, 2009

Natrona County Public Library – Youth Services Staff: "Milstead Award" Youth and Children's Literature, 2008

Bill Nelson: Distinguished Service Award, 2008

Natrona County Public Library – Children's Department: "Milstead Award" Youth and Children's Literature, 2006

Kate Mutch: Librarian of the Year, 2006

John Jorgensen: Meritorious Service Award, 2006

Emily Daly: Unsung Heroine, 2005

Greta Lehnerz: "Award" Award, 2004

Jerry Jones: Librarian of the Year, 2003

Carol McMurry: Meritorious Service Award, 2001

Casper Journal: Media Support Award, 2000

Casper Breakfast Optimist Club: Meritorious Service Award, 1996

Marsha Bradbury: Nora Van Burgh Professional Development Grant, 1993

Betty Ouderkirk, Wilma Bovie, and the Friends of the Library: Meritorious Service Award, 1991

Natrona County Public Library – Children's Department: "Milstead Award" Youth and Children's Literature, 1989

Agnes Hand: Trustee Citation, 1989

Natrona County Public Library: "Milstead Award" Youth and Children's Literature, 1984

Natrona County School District #1 Board of Trustees: Trustee Citation, 1983

Friends of the Library: Meritorious Service Award, 1981

Natrona County Public Library: "Milstead Award" Youth and Children's Literature, 1979

Appendix Four:
2008-2009 Annual Report

10 July 2009

From: Director, Natrona County Public Library
To: Natrona County Public Library Board of Trustees

Subj: Natrona County Public Library Annual Report 2008-2009

Attached is the Natrona County Public Library Annual Report for the period

1.   July 2008 through 30 June 2009.

2.   We have accomplished much during this year. Our most notable accomplishments include:

-   Checked out 630,899 items, up 93% since FY2001

-   368,852 people visited NCPL, up 7% over FY2008

-   Conducted a campaign for a new library which appeared as an expiring 6th cent sale tax measure on the 4 November 2008 ballot

-   Children's Department received WLA's 2008 Milstead Award

-   Presented 634 programs for NCSD #1

-   3,046 youth and 890 adults participated in the 2008 summer reading program

-   Presented 162 adult programs

-   74,737 Internet sessions were logged for a total of 47,542 hours

-   Issued an updated Community Profile and posted it online

Details of our FY2009 operations are attached. We continue to improve service on the solid foundation you have created.

3.   Thank you for the opportunity to serve the citizens of Natrona County in FY2009.

Respectfully,

Bill Nelson
Director

Enclosure Copy to: BOCC
                                    NCPL Foundation
                                    Friends of NCPL
                                    WY State Library
                                    City of Casper
                                    NCSD #1

OPERATING RESULTS

- Number of checkouts: 630,889, up 4.5%
- Number of patron visits: 368,852, up 7%
- Collection Turnover Rate: 3.45
- Number of Card Holders: 35,448
- Number of cards used this year: 15,788
- Number of new materials added: 21,390
- Number of Homepage Visits: 86,530

Community Outreach

- Quarterly "Community Builder" newsletter continued, funded by the NCPL Foundation as a strategic marketing resource.
- Continued regular bi-monthly articles in the Casper Journal; library articles were included in the *Casper Star-Tribune,* Our Town Casper, Literacy Volunteers Newsletter, Town of Mills Newsletter, Chamber of Commerce Newsletter, The Outrider, MPLA Newsletter and the Homeschooler's Newsletter.
- Radio PSAs were developed and aired throughout the year; multiple radio interviews conducted through Clear Channel Radio; on-air TV interviews by several staff with Channels 13 and K2.
- Began developing a "value-added" marketing campaign to reinforce NCPL's importance to our community.
- Hosted displays by local organizations including: Audubon Wyoming, Cent$ible Nutrition, Casper Photography Association, Casper Needle Guild, UW Art Museum, Friends of the Library, NCSD #1 Art Show & Central Wyoming Philatelic Association (Stamp Club).
- Participated in Homeless Project with NCSD #1, providing library cards for homeless students to check out up to 3 books. Replacements for materials lost through use of these cards are funded by the Casper Rotary Club.
- Participated in the Fair & Rodeo parade, winning 2nd place in the decorated vehicle category (8 Jul 08), and Christmas Light Parade (22 Nov 08).
- Provided performance space, bookmobile service and library information for families and students during the first NCSD #1 Back to School Bash (16 Aug 08).
- Hosted an information table featuring library materials and services at the Wyoming Women's Expo (3-4 Oct 08).
- Held "Food for Fines" (30 Nov-14 Dec 08); collected 1,193 non-perishable food items for Joshua's Storehouse (local food pantry).
- NCPL sponsored a session with Dr. Kathleen Kovner Kline entitled "Hardwired to Connect: The Social, Moral and Spiritual Foundations of Child Well-Being" at the Wyoming Methamphetamine and Substance Abuse Conference (7-8 Jan 09). Several NCPL staff members attended.
- Director presented Endowment Challenge Fundraising Program at the ALA Midwinter Conference in Denver (23 Jan 09).
- Provided two judges for Boy Scouts of America Snow Sculptures contest on Casper Mountain (31 Jan 09).
- Hosted the NCSD #1 Elementary Art Show "Art Through the Ages" (9 Apr –8 May 09).
- Met with 115th FIRES Brigade leadership regarding deployment of over 200 Natrona County service members and services the library can offer to their families; Purchased ad in *Casper Star-Tribune* special edition (12 Apr 09) in support of troops & families.
- Hosted Display: City of Casper Proposed Beech Street Modifications for public viewing and comment (May 09).

Youth Services Outreach

- Participated as a partner in the Wyoming Early Childhood Partnership grant (WYECP) for the purpose of improving services to young children in our community.
- Provided outreach programs for UWCC Humanities & Casper College Children's Literature Classes, NCSD #1 Professional Development/Fabulous Recreational Enrichment Days (FRED), Reading Is Fundamental (RIF), and Juvenile Detention Center.
- Provided Live Homework Help demonstration for NCSD #1 Elementary Library staff.

- Provided brochures on parenting topics to the school district's Family Resource Centers.
- Provided After School and School's Out programs for Boys & Girls Clubs.
- Provided storytime at Platte River Parkway Fall Festival for 28 attendees.
- Early Literacy Outreach included either library visits or storytimes provided for Early Head Start, Head Start and Neighborhood Child Learning Center.
- Provided storytimes for "I-Reach" and "Independent Opportunities" adults with developmental disabilities.
- Provided tours for Cub Scout packs, Girl Scout troops, and Home School Co-op.
- Provided library resource table at Raising Readers Bookfeast/Fest (20 Sep 08).
- Provided a children's booth with activities at the Hunting and Fishing Expo (11-13 Sep 08).
- Provided children's booth at Blue Envelope Health Fair (28 Mar 09).
- Youth Services Manager attended Central Oregon Early Literacy Conference (9 May 09).
- Youth Services Manager wrote "Parenting With Purpose" article for Natrona County Prevention Coalition's column, published in the *Casper Star-Tribune* (9 Jun 09).
- Teen librarian visited Dean Morgan, Centennial, Kelly Walsh High School, Star Lane High School, Roosevelt High School, Casper Classical Academy, St. Anthony's, University Park, Fort Caspar Academy, Park Elementary, Paradise Valley Elementary, Frontier Middle School, Manor Heights, and Southridge schools, providing programs and library information to 1,285 students. Visits included 21 Fabulous Recreational Enrichment Days (FRED) programs reaching 631 students.
- Teen Librarian served on boards for the Natrona County Prevention Coalition and the Safe Schools, Healthy Students grant administered by NCSD #1.
- Teen crafts created during "CrafTeen Give" programs were distributed to the library's Books By Mail homebound patrons.

Adult Services Outreach

- Reference librarians served on the Literacy Volunteers of Casper Board, Meth Conference Committee, Parenting Committee and Safe Schools, Healthy Students Grant Steering Committee.
- Reference librarians attended various community meetings including: County Commission, Casper City Council, Senior Center, Senior Network, Natrona County Prevention Coalition, Women's Business Roundtable and Meals on Wheels.
- Provided computer classes for CLIMB Wyoming (1, 8, 15, 22, 29 Oct 08) serving 30 participants and for I-Reach adults with disabilities (24 Feb & 10 Mar 09) serving 17 participants.
- Presented Read Aloud programs for I-Reach and Independent Opportunities (adults with disabilities).
- Reference librarian spoke about "Books by Mail" program at the Senior Center (21 Jan 09).
- Reference librarian spoke at AAUW meeting regarding Casper Area Boomer Study and NCPL involvement (14 Apr 09).
- Reference librarian presented information about NCPL's general and business services to Leadership Casper class (16 Apr 09).

Programs

- National Library Week (12-18 Apr 09): County Commission issued a Proclamation. Events included book discussion, Donna Kennedy author visit, Teen Poetry Slam, Legislative Forum, Elementary Art Show Reception, Family Movie & Pizza Night, and Bilingual Storytime.
- NCPL continued its agreement with Movie Licensing USA: 32 movies presented during the past 12 months. Several "film series" held: Epic Films, School's Out, Movie & Pizza, Holiday Movies and Independent Films.

Youth Services Programs

- Strong NCSD #1 interaction continued:
  - Developed and conducted 142 library programs in the schools (3,760 students)
  - Provided 492 Fabulous Recreational Enrichment Days (FRED) programs (13,220 students) formerly known as Professional Development
  - 69 classes visited NCPL (1,932 students).

- Over 2,490 children participated in the 2008 Summer Reading Program – "Catch the Reading Bug @ Your Library." Visiting performers included: Wayne & Wingnut, Magician Cody Landstrom, Dragons are Too Seldom Puppet Productions, Puppeteer Patti Smithsonian, Magician Ann Lincoln and Presto the Magician. Over 556 Teens participated in "Metamorphosis @ Your Library."
- 970 Natrona County first graders participated in Wyoming Reads at NCPL and the NIC (19 May 09); 189 received NCPL cards. Every Wyoming county participated in this year's Wyoming Reads program, with a total of over 7,200 participants. Over 225 individual schools from the state's 48 school districts brought students to 35 regional celebration locations.
- 134 children's storytime programs conducted with a total of 3,434 children and adults attending.
- 37 Tiny Tot Storytime programs with a total of 1,440 children and adults attending.
- Continued regular storytimes at Mills Branch Library: 46 sessions held with a total of 742 attending.
- Continued monthly Bilingual Storytimes in partnership with NCSD #1 Title III program (11 Jul 08, 25 Jul 08, 5 Nov 08, 3 Dec 08, 7 Feb 09, 21 Mar 09, 18 Apr 09, 16 May 09). Participated in Title III family program for Spanish speakers at North Casper School (29 Jan 09)
- Reading Is Fundamental (RIF) Program: 3,259 books distributed primarily to 2nd & 5th Graders in 13 schools during 93 separate programs.
- "After School @ the Library" continued Wednesdays throughout the school year. Programs included: Jack Prelutsky Party, Medieval Times, Smart Investing for Kids, Turkey Shoot Word Challenge, Acting Up! drama program, Chinese New Year, We the People, Follow the Money, Earth Day, and Fun with Curious George (32 sessions with 1,034 total attendees).
- Held 17 "After School/School's Out" programs for elementary age youth at the Mills Branch Library with 465 students attending.
- Programs for the "Tween" age-group (grades 4-6) were continued and included book clubs, after-school events, movie nights and a monthly Tween Advisory Group to help choose events.
- Implemented "We the People" grant from the National Endowment for the Humanities by including the "Created Equal" theme in FRED programs, After School @ the Library program, Tween Book discussion, teen "Read the Movie See the Book" event.
- Conducted "No Girls Allowed" programs: 8 sessions with a total of 115 boys attending.
- "Spooky Storytime" held in conjunction with downtown "Trick or Treat" (25 Oct 08).
- Hosted in-service day with Karen Czarnik (storytelling, crafts & drama) for Wyoming children's librarians and educators (6 Feb 09) with 46 attendees from around the state.
- Read Across America held with 182 attendees (2 Mar 09); Casper College Children's Literature class helped conduct this program.
- Co-sponsored with NCSD #1 a family program, "Learn to Draw in 3-D" with art instructor Mark Kistler. (22 Apr 09).
- Celebrated Children's Book Week with "Bedtime! Booktime!" (12 May 09).
- Began 2009 Summer Reading Programs: Children –"Be Creative @ Your Library"; Teens – "Express Yourself @ Your Library."
- Teen programming included: "Breaking Dawn" release party, Smart Investing for Teens, Read the Movie: See the Book, Teen Advisory Group, Poetry Slams, Game On! with Dance Dance Revolution, Guitar Hero and Rock Band, Hanging of the Greens, Teen Book Club, Afternoon Book Club, Teen Movie Nights, Anime Club and craft programs.
- Completed first round of a Great Stories Club grant from the American Library Association. Two titles distributed and 12 book club meetings held at Roosevelt High School reaching 519 students (Sep-Dec 08).
- Began second round of Great Stories Club grant from ALA (Jan 09). Three titles distributed and 13 meetings held reaching 396 Roosevelt High School students.
- Celebrated Teen Read Week (12-18 Oct 08); Held Teen Dinner & a Movie (10 Oct 08), YA Poetry Slam (14 Oct 08) and Magnetic Poetry Workshop (14 Oct 08).
- "Let's Talk College" events developed in partnership with the UW/CC Educational Opportunities Center targeted college-bound Teens and adults (28 Oct 08, 22 Jan 09 and 26 Mar 09).
- Celebrated Teen Tech Week (8-14 Mar 09); Held Teen Movie Night (6 Mar 09), Game On (10 Mar 09), and Open Mic Night (12 Mar 09).

Adult Services Programs

- Over 890 adults participated in the 2008 Summer Reading Program, "Don't Bug Me! I'm reading."
- 162 total Adult Programs with 3,104 people in attendance.
- Substance Abuse Prevention initiatives:
  - Provided informational pamphlets via displays at NCPL.
  - Events promoting healthy and stable families included Five Love Languages: Empowering couples (8 Nov 08); Family Game Night (19 Feb 09); Child Abuse Awareness Training (23 Feb 09); Family Movie & Pizza Night (17 Apr 09); The Muses: Family concert (25 Jun 09) and Bimonthly Bunco Nights for Families.
- Service to Seniors initiatives:
  - "Books-by-Mail" program increased from 50 to 61 participants.
  - Offered workshop for employers about "Retaining the Older Worker" (20 Oct 08) in response to Casper Area Boomer Study showing many boomers will remain working into their senior years.
  - Volunteer Income Tax Assistance made available to seniors and other citizens (6, 13, 20, 27 Feb & 6, 13 Mar 09).
  - Events for Seniors included Epic Film Series (15, 22, 29 Aug and 5, 12 Sep 08); Smart Investing for Seniors (18 Sep 08); Champions Mentoring Program (10 Oct 08); Medicare Part D Open Enrollment Assistance (16 Dec 08); Elderhostel Introduction (20 Jan & 17 Mar 09); Wellness Series covering a variety of health topics (5, 26 Feb, 3 Mar, 5 May, 4 Jun 09); and When I'm 64: Local resources for seniors & retirees (29 May 09).
- Implemented first half of a "Smart Investing" series sponsored through a grant from the Financial Industry Regulatory Authority (FINRA):
  - Purchased library materials regarding investments and personal finance.
  - Developed a webpage and handouts featuring additional resources.
  - Events included Smart Investing for Seniors (18 Sep 08); Basic Financial Planning (25 Sep 08); Investing in Stocks, Bonds & Mutual Funds (2 Oct 08); Investing for Retirement (9 Oct 08); Estate Planning / Money & Happiness (16 Oct 08); and Smart Investing programs for children (8 Oct 08), Tweens (11 Oct 08) and Teens (30 Oct 08).
- Responded to the declining national economic situation:
  - Affirmed the library's role in our community through a Casper Journal article "Your Library: A Money-Saver in Tough Times" (7 Jan 09).
  - Cosponsored Surviving Tough Times workshop for small businesses with the Wyoming Small Business Administration (13 Jan 09).
  - Offered Job Search Skills computer classes beginning in May 09.
- Authors spoke at NCPL: Gary Janski, poet (21 Jan 09); Donna Kennedy, Wyoming author (14 Apr, 09).
- Workshops to support businesses held in partnership with the Small Business Administration included Gro-Biz Government Contract Opportunities (25 Sep 08); Retaining the Older Worker (20 Oct 08); Surviving Tough Times for Small Businesses (13 Jan 09); Business Plan Workshop (24 Feb 09); and Free Money, Fact or Fiction? (20 Apr 09).
- Legislative Forum was held in partnership with the League of Women Voters (15 Apr 09); Legislators discussed post-legislature issues.
- Adult book group met 14 Jul 08, 11 Aug 08, 8 Sep 08, 13 Oct 08, 10 Nov 08, 8 Dec 08, 12 Jan 09, 9 Feb 09, 9 Mar 09, 13 Apr 09 and 11 May 09.
- Mystery book discussion group began 28 Jan 09 and met 25 Feb 09, 25 Mar 09, 22 Apr 09, 27 May 09, and 24 Jun 09.
- Other adult programs offered: Independent Film Series (22 Jul 08, 26 Aug 08, 23 Sep 08, 28 Oct 08, 25 Nov 08, 23 Dec 08, 20 Jan 09, 17 Feb 09, 10 Mar 09, 21 Apr 09, 19 May 09, 16 Jun 09); "The Beats" book and film discussions, funded by Wyoming Humanities Council (28 Jul 08, 25 Aug 08, 28 Aug 08); Papermaking Workshop (9 Aug 08); Wyoming Musician Bryan Ragsdale (15 Sep 08); Grid-Tied Solar Energy (6 Oct 08); The Bronze Art of Chris Navarro (13 Oct 08); Off-Grid Solar Energy (30 Oct 08); How's Your Credit? Workshop (3 Nov 08); Solar-Thermal Energy (17 Nov 08); Christmas Cardmaking (4 Dec 08); Breaking Into the Music Business (4 Dec 08); Gingerbread House Workshops (6, 13 Dec 08); Holiday Film Series (7, 14, 21 Dec 08); Learn About the Peace Corps (11 Dec 08);The Muses concerts (16 Jan 09, 25 Jun 10); ADHD Workshop (14 Mar 09).

- Introductory computer classes offered for Computers, Internet, MS Word, Excel, PowerPoint, Publisher, Online Gaming, Online Dating, Genealogy, Online Health Information, Website Evaluation, Blogging, Web 2.0, Ebay, Google, Downloadable Audio & Video, Wyoming Newspaper Archive and Job Search Skills; trained 446 people during 61 classes.
- Began "Be Creative @ Your Library" 2009 Adult Summer Reading Program.

Library Collection

- NCPL system circulation for FY09 was 630,899 up 4.5% from the previous year; up 93% since FY2001.
- Added 21,390 items to the collection; total items in the collection 182,920.
- Conspectus reports generated and used for managing collections.
- Increased collection on substance abuse prevention, parenting skills and personal finance.
- Continued hosting the "Fundraising Resource Center", a service of the Foundation Center, which includes reference books and databases to aid grant seekers. This service is funded by the NCPL Foundation.
- Continued Live Homework Help, an online tutoring service now available to K-12 and adult learners from 3-9 p.m.; funded by the Natrona County Recreation Joint Powers Board. During FY09, 319 students used the service.
- Prototype bin developed to ease browsing of easy readers in Youth Services Department.
- 500 Parent Education Network DVDs purchased and distributed to parents during 2009 Summer Reading programs.
- Began actively collecting yearbooks from area schools.
- PSL developed shelving plan to accommodate collection growth over the coming 4 years.
- Digital newspaper project rolled out by the Wyoming State Library making Wyoming newspapers between 1849-1922 available in a searchable digital format. NCPL began classes and one-on-one training for this resource.

Other Successes

- Children's Department received WLA's 2008 Milstead Award for program excellence for children (2 Oct 08).
- Director received WLA's 2008 Distinguished Service Award (2 Oct 08)
- Over 2,200 items processed through Tech Services in the month of April 09, a major milestone.
- Youth Services Department received a "We the People" grant from the National Endowment for the Humanities in May 09 with the theme "Picturing America" to be implemented in FY 10.
- Received $24,000 from the Natrona County Recreation Joint Powers Board for the 2009 Summer Reading Program.
- Received a $2,000 Early Literacy Grant from Target for infant/toddler summer reading component, implemented during 2009 Summer Reading Programs.
- Walter Jones completed research and began writing a book documenting NCPL's first 100 years. His work will be completed during FY10 and is funded by the Friends of the Library.

OPERATIONS
Library Administration

- Board Officers for FY09: Chris Mullen, President; Charles Robertson, Vice President; Mary Ann Collins, Secretary; Randy Buffington, Treasurer; and Harper Park.
- A Committee considered the implications of purchasing food for programs with public funding; Friends of the Library agreed to fund $4,000 annually for food associated with library programs.
- Made plans to look at the possibility of expanding Childrens Department into the Crawford Room; began investigating the effects of loss or partial loss of the Crawford Room due to this anticipated expansion.
- Use of the Crawford Room by a Buddhist group whose advertising showed intent to proselytize was denied in accordance with county policy. Fielded media questions related to this action.
- Fielded media questions regarding the Consumer Product Safety Improvement Act (CPSIA) passed by Congress in Oct 08 regarding testing for lead in children's books, originally to take effect in Feb 2009 and now postponed to Feb 2010.
- Staff In-Service Day (13 Aug 08) featured Warren Graham, author of "The Black-Belt Librarian."
- Assistant Children's Librarian Glenda Williams retired after 18 years of service (27 Aug 08).
- Bookmobile made a trip to Billings (mid-August 08) for warranty work.
- Provided update to County Commission (23 Sep 08, 24 Feb 09); briefed new Commissioner Ed Opella (10 Dec 08).
- Director and Press Stephens (WCF) conducted Fundraising Program at WLA Post-Conference seminar (4 Oct 08).

- Director attended Wyoming Library Directors' Retreat in Thermopolis (11-12 Sep 08).
- Began collecting "tough reference questions of the week" (Jan 09).
- A fundraising training luncheon was held as staff development for degreed librarians (14 Jan 09).
- Issued an updated Community Profile (Mar 09); copies distributed to over 100 community leaders and organizations and posted on the NCPL website.
- Board began a cycle of routine policy reviews in May 09 which will continue through the coming fiscal year.
- Two staff attended the WyLD annual meeting in Dubois (18-19 Jun 09).

Library Technology

- 74,737 patron Internet sessions were logged for a total of 47,542 hours.
- Replaced old staff server with new computer (Jun 09).
- Replaced 10 staff computers and upgraded memory in 7 to support new version of Workflows.

Facilities

- Removed the light post illuminating Prometheus after it failed during a wind storm.
- Installed 2 new external surveillance cameras.
- Friends of the Library painted and reorganized basement in order to host future book sales without using Crawford Room.
- Attempts to sell or relocate compact shelving into new courthouse were unsuccessful.
- Added shelving units throughout library to accommodate growing collection.
- Replaced air conditioning unit for Children's Department.

New Library Project

- On 19 June 2008 (last fiscal year) the Trustees voted to put forward the following language on the 4 November 2008 ballot:

  "For a new public library; shall Natrona County be authorized to impose an additional one percent (1%) Specific Purpose Sales and Use Tax, within Natrona County, for the purpose of acquiring property, building a new library with equipment and appropriate parking, located in central Casper in order to expand literacy, education, programs and services for all citizens; this tax shall raise $43,250,000.00, at which time the Specific Purpose Sales and Use Tax will expire; any excess tax funds and interest thereon shall be used for operation and maintenance or construction of the new library and all funds will be subject to an annual audit."

- The total cost of the 96,000 square feet project had the following costs:

Construction	$30.50 Million
Land acquisition	$3.75 Million
Operation, equipment, and books	$9.00 Million
Total	$43.25 Million

- Trustees visited all six towns, cities, and the County Commission to seek ballot approval. By late August 2008 all six municipalities and the Commission approved placing the project on the ballot.
- Informational Outreach and Meetings:
  - Director or other library staff spoke about the new library at the 5 Trails Rotary Club (10 Jul 08); American Society of Women Accountants (19 Aug 09); Casper Young Professionals Network (9 Sep 08); League of Women Voters (4 Oct 08); Natrona County Prevention Coalition (7 Oct 08); AAUW (14 Oct 08); Alpha Delta Kappa (11 Oct 08);
  - Public input meetings conducted (2 Jul 08, 16 Sep 08, 30 Sep 08, 11 Oct 08, 14 Oct 08, 21 Oct 08, 29 Oct 08) at the main library, (22 Oct 08) at the Mills branch, and (23 Oct 08) at the Midwest High School.
  - Produced 2 informational inserts distributed through the Casper Journal to all Natrona County households (17 Sep 08 & 15 Oct 08).
  - Informational materials distributed via information booths at the Hunting and Fishing Expo (11-13 Sep 08), Equality State Book Fest (20 Sep 08), Raising Readers Bookfeast/Fest (Sep 08), Wyoming Women's Expo (3-4 Oct 08) and Friends of the Library Fall Booksale (25-26 Oct 08).
- A PAC, "Citizens for a New Library" was created on 14 March 2008. Initial leadership was not forthcoming in planning and fundraising. Efforts to recast PAC leadership and action began in June 2008. Ginny Garner became the PAC Director. The new group developed a Fundraising & Administration Committee, a Field Operations Committee, and a Public Relations Committee. The PAC raised approximately $60,000 and developed considerable marketing materials.

- Three surveys were conducted during the campaign. The Trustees commissioned two telephone surveys (statistically accurate to 5%). The first, conducted by Chilenski Strategy Group in February 2008 indicated 67.3% would vote "Definitely/Probably Yes", 26.2% "Definitely/Probably No". A follow-up survey conducted by Chilenski in early July after the project costs were known indicated 55% would vote "Definitely/Probably Yes", 33% "Definitely/Probably No", 13% "No Opinion". The *Casper Star-Tribune* commissioned a Mason-Dixon Poll of 400 likely voters between 13-15 October. Their survey yielded the following results reported in the 21 October 2008 newspaper: 48% "for", 39% "against" and 13% "Undecided".
- Results of the 4 November 2008 election were 15,579 votes (48%) "for" and 17,132 votes (52%) "against" the new library.
- Proposed reasons for the defeat vary, but the most significant cause was the marked downturn in the national economy during September-October 2008. This dramatic market sell-off and the associated national media coverage generated fear and uncertainty in the local electorate… and an unwillingness to service a new sales tax. Additional actions that could have helped the campaign include:
  - The need for a new library being more obvious
  - Visibly supportive County Commissioners
  - Publicly active Trustees
  - Improved Friends/grass roots advocacy
- Groathouse Construction developed the construction cost estimates in early June. In retrospect, this was near the peak of the construction cost cycle. Construction costs noticeably declined shortly thereafter when the national economy collapsed in September-October 2008. Groathouse Construction indicated that construction costs declined about 7.5% by early December 2008 from the June peak, mostly due to material cost decreases.
- A lessons-learned file was created for use in a future capital campaign.

Library Support Organizations

Foundation:
- Completed raising matching funds in the "Public Libraries Endowment Challenge Match" in the Wyoming Legislature. NCPL received 1:1 matching funds of $295,652.
- Sponsored their last Edible Book Fest at NCPL (1 Apr 09); this program will be funded by the Friends in the future.
- Received $1 million from Susie and Mick McMurry (6 Nov 08), showing their support of NCPL.
- Beth Worthen, Executive Director, nominated for the *Casper Star-Tribune* "40 under 40" recognition.

Friends:
- Fall Book Sale was held (25-26 Oct 08); Spring Book Sale was held (28 Mar – 4 Apr 09).
- Friends Spaghetti Dinner held (13 Nov 08) with local author Ken Kreckel as speaker.
- Friends surpassed a cumulative revenue of $1 million from their 38 years of book sale operations.
- Friends provided $35,000 to the Foundation to complete the endowment challenge match program.
- Friends indicate they intend to develop a library advocacy role in the future.
- Friends repainted and reoriented shelving in the basement in anticipation of holding future sales in this work room.

Volunteers:
- 256 individuals volunteered during the past year for a total of 1,420 volunteer hours in FY09.
- Volunteers participated in: Adopt-a-Shelf, book repair, ILL mailing, Art Show help, Wyoming Reads helpers, YA helpers, A/V assistants, bulletin board creation, holds calling, mailings, Tech Services help, parade help and book cleaning.

Staff Association:
- Selected the following as NCPL Quarterly Local Heroes: Barb Cornia (Sep 08), Nancy Witzeling (Dec 08), Friends of the Library (Mar 09), Woods Learning Center 6th & 7th grade classes (Jun 09).
- Approved purchase of 4 advertisements in support of New Library project – ad funds were raised by individual donations (Oct 08).
- Staff picnic on 10 Aug 08 at Sunrise Bowling Alley.
- Christmas party on 7 Dec 08 at the Goose Egg Inn.

SHORT-TERM GOALS (2010-2012)

Library Services

- Develop and implement library services that will help reduce the dropout rate, prevent substance abuse, and serve an aging population.
- Continue to increase NCPL's presence in NCSD #1 classrooms.
- Continue to develop more library services/programs/interaction with Teens.
- Increase collection size in accordance with the Collection Development Plan.
- Promote literacy and education in the community, especially for boys.

Administration

- Continue implementing the 2006-2010 strategic plan.
- Continue to foster closer communications with County Commissioners, City of Casper, and other municipal entities and individuals.
- Complete book about NCPL history.
- Plan and execute a celebration for NCPL's 100th anniversary, May 2010.
- Support staff and Board member attendance at library conferences and educational opportunities.

Facilities

- Continue to build awareness and support for a new main library including:
  - Making the need for a new library more obvious.
  - Building visible and active County Commissioners support.
  - Trustees engaging political/civic groups to be supportive.
  - Creating an active advocacy role within the Friends organization.

LONG-TERM GOALS (2013+)

- Build a new library facility.
- Achieve at least average Wyoming per-capita funding; provide stable source of public revenue.

Works Consulted

Note: Items without publisher or repository are held in the Natrona County Public Library archives.

Agreement. Natrona County Library and Westronics, Inc. September 29, 1971.

"Annual Report of the Natrona County Public Library." 1928-1945 (calendar year).

"Annual Report of the Natrona County Public Library." 1945-1969 (calendar year).

Babcock, Charlotte M. "Casper's Library." 6-page typed manuscript. No date.

Beach, Mrs. Alfred H. (Cora M.). *Women of Wyoming*. Casper, Wyoming: S. E. Boyer & Co. 1927.

Bid letters. E. G. Ericksen & Son, August 19, 1933; John Jourgensen Paints, August 17, 1933; L. D. Leisinger, August 19, 1933; M. R. Davis, no date; Redwine Building Company; August 18, 1933.

Bille, Ed. *Early Days at Salt Creek and Teapot Dome*. Casper, Wyoming: Mountain States Lithograph Company. 1978.

Boughton, Lesley D. "Application for LSTA Title II Construction and Technology Enhancements." 2-page form with attachments. April 11, 1997.

Burke, Margaret. "Wyoming Library Builds Addition," *Library Journal*. 80/4 (February 15, 1955): 427-428.

Burnidge Cassell Associates (BCA). "Natrona County Public Library – Casper, Wyoming: Conceptual Site Plan C-3." 1-sheet, June 10, 2008.

Burnidge Cassell Associates (BCA). "View From the Northwest – (First Street)." 1 sheet. No date.

Carnegie correspondence regarding the Natrona County Public Library: Harold Bryant Brooks, Wilson S. Kimball, Frank W. Mondell, M. P. Wheeler to Andrew Carnegie; James Bertram to Bryant B. Brooks, Alex Butler, Wilson S. Kimball, Frank W. Mondell, M. P. Wheeler. Wilson S. Kimball to C. A. Randall. C. A. Randall to Mayor and City Council [town of Casper].

Casper Rotary Foundation and Downtown Development Authority. "Art for the Streets: Self-Guided Tour to Casper's Public Sculpture." Casper, Wyoming. No date.

Certificate of Incorporation of the Natrona County Library Association, September 9, 1909.

Citizens for a New Library. "Natrona County Public Library: Building for our Community's Future." 1-page flyer. No date.

Conversation. Walter Jones with Bill Nelson. July 11, 2008.

Crawford, James G. 1 page typed manuscript regarding LaFrances Sullivan, August 13, 1969.

Dowlin, Kenneth E. "A Summary Report of the Activities of the Natrona County Public Library in Its Use of CATV to Provide Library Services." 2-page typed manuscript. November 1, 1972.

Dowlin, Kenneth E. "A Summary Report of the Activities of the Natrona County Public Library in Its Use of CATV to Provide Library Services." 2-page typed manuscript. December 15, 1974.

Email. Beverly Diehl to Walter Jones. September 26, 2008.

Email. Bill Nelson to Walter Jones. November 17, 2008.

Email. Bill Nelson to Walter Jones. February 25, 2009.

Email. Bill Nelson to Walter Jones. February 26, 2009.

Email. Bill Nelson to Walter Jones. February 27, 2009.

Email. Bill Nelson to Walter Jones. March 10, 2009.

Email. Bill Nelson to Walter Jones. April 25, 2009.

Email. Bill Nelson to Walter Jones. July 4, 2009.

Email. Bill Nelson to Walter Jones. July 6, 2009.

Email. Bill Nelson to Walter Jones. July 11, 2009.

Email. Bill Nelson to Walter Jones. July 18, 2009.

Email. Bill Nelson to Walter Jones. July 27, 2009.

Email. Bill Nelson to Walter Jones. December 4, 2009.

Email. Frank Schepis to Walter Jones. August, 12, 2009.

Email. Greta Lehnerz to Walter Jones. January 23, 2009.

Email. Greta Lehnerz to Walter Jones. January 26, 2009.

Email. Jackie Read to Walter Jones. March 23, 2009.

Fillerup, Grace. *Let Your Light Shine: Pioneer Women Educators of Wyoming.* Delta Kappa Gamma. 1965.

"First Record Book of Natrona County Public Library." August 7, 1909-December 10, 1926.

Floor plans. Carnegie Library [Natrona County Public Library] and Natrona County Public Library Addition. 1925.

Frech, Sue. "Adult Services at Natrona County Public Library" 1-page fact sheet. Library Scrapbook. 1968.

Friends of the Library Scrapbook. Publicity, Book Sales. 1972-1989.

Garbutt, Irving and Chuck Morrison. *Casper Centennial, 1889-1989; Natrona County, Wyoming, 1890-1990.* Dallas, Texas: Curtis Media Corporation. 1990.

Hemry, Kathleen. *Kathleen's Book: An Album of Early Pioneer Wyoming in Word and Pictures.* Casper, Wyoming: Mountain States Lithographing. 1988.

Hill, Karen. "Report: Studio Advisory Board." 3-page typed manuscript. May 19, 1980.

Interview. Walter Jones with Beverly Diehl. August 8, 2008.

Interview. Walter Jones with Jerry Hand. November 21, 2006.

Interview. Walter Jones with Trula Cooper, Frank "Pinky" Ellis, and Art Volk. January 20, 2007.

Johnson, J. W. "Natrona County Library Notes." Typed manuscript. No date.

Jones, Christopher. "A Summary Report of the Activities of the Natrona County Public Library in Its Use of CATV to Provide Library Services." 2-page typed manuscript. November 15, 1976.

Jones, Theodore. *Carnegie Libraries Across America: A Public Legacy.* New York: John Wiley & Sons, Inc. 1997.

Jones, Walter. *History of the Sand Bar: 1888-1977.* Casper, Wyoming: BASO, Inc. 1981.

King, Robert A. *Trails to Rails: A History of Wyoming's Railroads.* Casper, Wyoming: Mountain States Lithographing. 2003.

Kukura, Edna G. and Susan Niethammer True. *Casper: A Pictorial History.* Norfolk, Virginia: The Donning Company. 1986.

Lease Agreement. Between the Midwest Refining Company and Natrona County Public Library Board. February 28, 1930.

Letter. Bill Nelson to Wm. Kevin O'Toole (USGPO). September 20, 2004.

Letter. Carolyn (Crawford) Bentzen to Editor, *Casper Star-Tribune.* September 30, 2000.

Letter. Charles Rose to Board of County Commissioners. October 13, 1948.

Letter. David Schroeder (Manna Media) to Bob Desai. April 8, 1980.

Letter. Dick Jay to Suzanne LeBarron. October 13, 1992.

Letter. Eleanor Davis to Mr. Jacobs [Joe P. Jacobs, member of the Natrona County Library Board of Trustees, 1927-1928]. March 15, 1928.

Letter. Harold Healey to J. W. Johnson. October 21, 1948.

Letter. Harold E. Meier to Janus Olsen. August 1, 1986.

Letter. James G. Crawford to Board of County Commissioners. [Date unreadable, possibly March 25, 1950.]

Letter. Janus Olsen to Pat McDonald. September 4, 1992.

Letter. John Albanese to Kenneth E. Dowlin. November 17, 1969.

Letter. Kenneth E. Dowlin to Mrs. James G. Crawford. October 30, 1972.

Letter. Lesley D. Boughton to Board of Directors. November 10, 1998.

Letter. Lesley D. Boughton to Christine N. Brady. September 18, 1995.

Letter. Lesley Boughton to Doug Cooper. May 15, 2000.

Letter. Librarian to Mr. Carl F. Shumaker, President, Natrona County Public Library Board. January 10, 1933.

Letter. Librarian to William H. Clift. January 31, 1935.

Letter. Pat McDonald to Lesley D. Boughton. March 2, 1993.

Letter. Sharyle Good to Ruth Adelman. February 7, 1995.

Letter. Wilson S. Kimball to Andrew Carnegie. June 12, 1905.

"Library Bond Issue Facts." 9-page typed manuscript with attached statistical sheet. [No date. Probably late 1966 or early 1967.]

"Library Bond Issue Facts." 10-page typed manuscript. [No date but prior to August 26, 1969.]

Mead, Jean. *Casper Country: Wyoming's Heartland.* Boulder, Colorado: Pruett Publishing Company, Inc. 1987.

Memo. Chris Jones to Library Board of Directors. No date.

Memo. Karen Hill to B. M. Desai. May 7, 1980.

Memo. Karen Hill to Library Board. May 8, 1981.

"Midwest Traveling Libraries," *Midwest Review 2* (January 1921): 11.

Minutes of Natrona County Library Board. November 22, 1927 – May 12, 1959.

Minutes of Natrona County Public Library Board. May 28, 1959 – March 10, 2009.

Mokler, Alfred James. *History of Natrona County, Wyoming: 1888-1922.* Casper, Wyoming: Mountain States Lithographing. 1989.

Natrona County High School Class of 1950. *Memories of Casper, 1935-1955.* Casper, Wyoming: Mountain States Lithographing. 2000.

"Natrona County Public Library Annual Report." 1999-2000 – 2008-2009.

Natrona County Public Library. "Crawford Receives National Library Award." News Release. June 5, 2000.

Natrona County Public Library. *Community Builder.* Volume 1, 2003 – volume 4, 2009.

Natrona County Public Library. "Notes & Quotes." September-November 1988.

Natrona County Public Library. "Welcome to Natrona County Public Library." Pamphlet. No date.

Natrona County Public Library. "Your Proposed New Library: Building for Our Community's Future." 4-page brochure. No date.

Natrona County Public Library scrapbook. "NCPL Clippings 1950 to 1967."

Natrona County Public Library scrapbook. "Children's Dept. Photo's & Clippings, 1937-1967."

Natrona County Public Library scrapbook. "1967: 50th Anniversary of Wyoming Flag: Also Honoring Mrs. Keyes."

Natrona County Public Library scrapbook. "1968."

Natrona County Public Library scrapbook. "1969."

Natrona County Public Library scrapbook. "John Cotton Dana. January 1 – December 31, 1969."

Natrona County Public Library System. "The Library's Future, Paying It Forward…" PowerPoint presentation. January 30, 2001.

Natrona County Tribune. March 16, November 2, December 14, 1905; February 13, 1907.

Nelson, Bill. "New Public Library summary." 2-page fact sheet. July 3, 2008.

Nelson, Bill. "News Release." Natrona County Public Library. 2-page typed manuscript. June 5, 2000.

Nelson, Bill. "Thoughts for the Next Election." 1-page sheet. November 7, 2008.

News Release. "Patent Trademark Library Relocates." February 28, 2001.

Newspapers. *Casper Daily Tribune, Casper Tribune Herald, Natrona County Tribune.*

No author. "A Brief History of the Johnson Memorial Studio." 1-page typed manuscript. No date.

No author. "Bookmobile Fact Sheet." 1-page typed manuscript. No date.

No author. "Goals and Objectives of the Natrona County Public Library." 10-page typed manuscript. October 19, 1970.

No author. "Schedule for Library Festival." 3-page typed manuscript. 1972.

No author. "Submission Guidelines for Bookmobile Exterior Design." Typed manuscript. 2004.

No author. "Wyoming Library Association Meritorious Service Award Nomination: John Jorgensen." No date.

No author. No title. Subject: Bookworm Club. 11-page typed manuscript. No date.

No author. No title. Subject: Opening library's new wing. 4-page typed manuscript. January 5, 1954.

No author. No title. Subject: 1950 Bond Issue. 3-page typed manuscript. No date.

Olsen, Kenneth. *Old Natrona County Court Houses.* Casper, Wyoming: Wyoming Field Science Foundation. 1975.

Progressive Men of the State of Wyoming. Chicago, Illinois: A. W. Bowen & Co. 1903.

"Prometheus: A Gift to the People of Natrona County." Plaque – located at front entrance to NCPL. No date.

"Public Library Statistical Report." [Form changed several times and NCPL occasionally changed from ALA approved form to Wyoming State Library form.] Natrona County Public Library. 1927-1945 (calendar year).

"Report of the Natrona County Public Library, Casper, Wyoming." 1928, 1929, and 1959-1960.

R. L. Polk Directory Company. *Casper City and Natrona County Directory.* Salt Lake City, Utah: R. L. Polk Directory Company. 1931-1932, 1939, 1941.

Roberts, Harold D. *Salt Creek, Wyoming: The Story of a Great Oil Field.* Denver, Colorado: Midwest Oil Corporation. 1956.

"Specifications of Additions and Alterations to Natrona County Library, Casper, Wyoming." Dubois & Goodrich Architects. [1925]

[State of Wyoming.] *Cumulated Annual Report: Wyoming Public Libraries.* 1983/84, 1984/85, 1986/87, 1988/89.

State of Wyoming. *Library Statistical Report.* 1946-1967.

State of Wyoming. *Wyoming Public Library: Annual Statistical Report Form.* 1969.

[State of Wyoming.] *Wyoming Public Library: Annual Activity Report Form.* June 30, 1973 – June 30, 1984.

[State of Wyoming.] *Wyoming Public Library Annual Statistical Report.* June 30, 1998 – June 30, 2003.

Technology Committee. "Interim NCPL Technology Center Plan: Recommendations." Typewritten manuscript. May 3, 2002.

Trenholm, Virginia Cole, ed. *Wyoming Blue Book.* (Vol. II). Cheyenne, Wyoming: Wyoming State Archives and Historical Department. 1974.

Van Slyck, Abigail A. *Free to All: Carnegie Libraries & American Culture: 1890-1920.* Chicago: University of Chicago Press. 1995.

"Wyoming's Carnegie Libraries." *Wyoming Library Roundup* (Winter 2007): 11-14.